9.99-

EFFECTIVE PROBLEM SOLVING

D0625457

BUSINESS & MANAGEMENT

EFFECTIVE PROBLEM SOLVING

How to understand the process and practise it successfully

Steven Kneeland

How To Books

British Library Cataloguing in Publication Data
A catalogue record for this book is available from the British Library.

© Copyright 1999 Steven Kneeland.

First published by How To Books Ltd, 3 Newtec Place,
Magdalen Road, Oxford OX4 1RE, United Kingdom.
Tel: (01865) 793806. Fax: (01865) 248780.
email: info@howtobooks.co.uk
www.howtobooks.co.uk

Note: The material contained in this book is set out in good faith for
general guidance and no liability can be accepted for loss or expense
incurred as a result of relying in particular circumstances on statements made
in the book. The laws and regulations are complex and liable to change, and
readers should check the current position with the relevant authorities before
making personal arrangements.

Produced for How To Books by Deer Park Productions.
Typeset by PDQ Typesetting, Stoke-on-Trent, Staffs.
Printed and bound by Cromwell Press, Trowbridge, Wiltshire.

Contents

List of Illustrations

Preface

I am confident that, when you finish reading this book, you will be a more effective problem-solver.

I say that because I am now writing the *preface*. The preface is the part of the book I decided to do *last*, and it won't get done until I am satisfied with the rest of the book. And being satisfied means being confident that, when you finish reading this book, you the reader will be a more effective problem-solver. Hence my opening statement.

In the following 13 chapters I cover the pragmatics of problem-solving. The realities. The things that make a difference in real-life business situations. Such as:

- Managing a crisis situation.
- Thinking strategically.
- Weighing the risks.
- Exercising business judgement.
- Trusting your instincts.
- Rallying support for a solution.
- Selling your ideas.
- Getting the whole team involved.

There are, hopefully, some good points to be made during the course of this book. Some genuinely useful insights to be passed along. Some good tools and techniques.

Where do they come from? On some occasions, the source is an expert of some standing – a Stephen Covey, for example, or a Lord Thomson, or someone who has written a classic article for the *Harvard Business Review*. Where appropriate, these sources have been duly acknowledged.

By and large, however, this book is built upon insights gleaned from managers like yourself, dealing with real issues and real problems. To capture something of the flavour of how real managers think, I have opted to include actual quotations throughout the book. At times, I am reporting what a manager once said to me, trying to remember the exact words as best I can. At other times, the quotation is part-real and part-invented ... a composite, representing a point that a *lot* of different managers have made.

To help things flow along more smoothly, I will ascribe these quotations to a group of five fictitious managers whom I will call the *Famous Five*.

- Jennifer Adair: Customer Service Manager with a London-based tour operator.

- Jack Carter: Director of the medical products division for a large manufacturer of industrial products.

- Tony Martindale: Director of Sales and Marketing for a leading packaged food company.

- Jill Pritchard: Columnist and author, working out of her home in Chipping Norton.

- Graeme Weir: Manufacturing director for a Leamington-based producer of automotive components.

Try to imagine these five individuals working along with us, as consultants and commentators. Five experienced and perceptive managers who all have – as we shall see – some very useful insights to offer.

A book – any book – is a collaborative effort. I have to acknowledge the encouragement, patience, support, and business-like assistance of Giles Lewis and Nikki Read. This book, hopefully, will be just one of many joint efforts to provide you – the business reader – with things that are honestly and truly worth reading.

On the home front, Pam and the kids – Jessica and Jennifer – have somehow resisted the temptation to throw both me and my computer into the duck pond that sits behind our house, and without their support and understanding this book ... could probably have been finished a lot sooner. But it wouldn't, I am sure, have been as good.

You, the reader, will have the final word. *Use* the book. Think of it as a tool. Something to be not just read but thought about, scribbled on, fiddled with, and hopefully added in a helpful fashion to your already existing storehouse of knowledge and insight. Will it actually make you a more effective problem-solver? Yes, I think it will.

Steven Kneeland

1
A Problem-solving Model

Problem-solving ability isn't about *intelligence*. It's about thinking straight. It's about *getting the process right*.

When you pay a mechanic to figure out what's making that funny noise under the bonnet of your car you probably don't spend too much time worrying about how *intelligent* he is. What you worry about is whether he has the right training and the right tools.

Our aim in this opening chapter is to build a **model** of the problem-solving process. Whether it's a mechanic working under the bonnet of our car or someone at the Bank of England deciding whether to raise interest rates by a point or two, all we can hope for is that the person has mastered the art of straight thinking.

WHAT IS A PROBLEM?

A problem is basically a deviation from the norm, serious enough to require correction. There is a gap between what *is* and what *ought to be*. Problem-solving is the process we use to bring these two elements back into alignment.

That's the formal definition. But let's recognise that the word 'problem' is a very general one. We might talk, for example, about the problem of unemployment in the North, or about not having a problem with the idea of a stranger joining us at our table in a crowded lunchtime pub.

For the benefit of this exercise we're situating you somewhere in the world of business – we'll assume a mid-level management role. And we're assuming further that a situation has come to or been brought to your attention.

Defining a problem
- There is a gap between the way things are and the way they should be.

- The gap concerns you as a manager. It is worth paying attention to.

- There is uncertainty about either what is causing the gap or how to close it.

- Something – or someone – is pressing for a solution.

- The situation is persistent. It is not going to go away all by itself.

The problem might be sharply defined, with clear-cut boundaries. Bill can't make the Tuesday meeting. Or, it might be fuzzy and amorphous. There are not enough people willing to break with tradition and challenge the status quo.

EXPLORING TWO TYPES OF PROBLEM

There are, in very broad strokes, two main types of problem that we will find ourselves dealing with.

1. The Fix-It Problem
A **Fix-It problem** is something that needs fixing.

- Profit contribution from our northwest region is running 10 per cent behind forecast.

- Radio Four's share of the afternoon listening audience was down by 5 per cent in the last survey.

- We had only five complaints from January through May and all of a sudden we've got three in one week.

In cases such as these, the fact that we've got a problem is quite obvious.

At other times – and this is perhaps, for someone in a managerial role at least, the more common situation – something is bothering us. It's still a **Fix-It** problem, but it's not clear-cut.

- I think the product line as a whole is showing its age. If we don't do something soon, we're dead.

- Your proposal contains some sound ideas, John, but there's not enough *excitement* in it.

- I'm not happy with the way Jim is performing. He ought to be one of my *stars* – not a bit-player.

> With a *Fix-It* problem the focus is on the *status quo* side of the gap and the message is 'Fix it'. *Make the problem go away.*

The 'gap' in such cases is between an undesirable state of affairs – *now* – and a desirable state of affairs in the *future*. In some cases, the mere *absence* of the troublesome state of affairs will do. Either way, the **problem** is that of fixing the *status quo*.

2. The Do-It Problem

The Do-It problem is a bit different. Rather than being faced with a 'problem' that has to be solved, we have set or are assigned a goal or objective to be achieved.

- The HR group has to have 25 new graduates hired by the end of July.

- George has decided – and he swears that this time he means business – to quit smoking.

- I'd like to see more people questioning things, asking *why*.

- The Stoke-on-Trent plant has been given the goal of reducing inventory costs by 10 per cent.

The 'gap' in this case is really between the present situation, which isn't necessarily 'bad' – and the outcome we want to achieve.
With a **Fix-It** problem the focus is on the *status quo* side of the gap and the message is 'Fix it'. *Make the problem go away.*

> With a *Do-It* problem, the focus is on the future state of affairs and the message is 'Do it'. *Move us in that direction.*

EXAMINING THE PROBLEM-SOLVING PROCESS

The **problem-solving process** is, in practice, as varied as the problems toward which it is directed.
Some problems we solve without even thinking about them. A package that was due to be mailed yesterday, and which absolutely *has* to be in the recipient's hands by tomorrow, wasn't quite ready for the afternoon pick-up at the post office. So we call the courier

company and arrange for it to be picked up for next-day delivery.
The reason we didn't have to think about it was because this kind of
thing had happened before.

The *first* time it happened, on the other hand, necessitated some
bona fide problem-solving. Do we get in the car and drive the
package to its destination? Or maybe there's a bus or train service
that's cheaper. But could they get it there by 10.00a.m. tomorrow?

Notice how one very important part of the problem-solving
process is setting priorities... deciding on what can give a bit and
what can't. The idea of calling the recipient and explaining that the
parcel would be arriving a day late was rejected. No, it's *got* to be
there by 10.00a.m. tomorrow. That's a small sub-decision we made.
It establishes a basic condition that has to be satisfied, and by so
doing it narrows the range of options considerably. It also helps
move the problem-solving process forward.

DEVELOPING A MODEL

Problem-solving is something that a lot of us take for granted. But
most of us haven't *trained* ourselves to be good problem-solvers or
given much thought to problem-solving as a process.

The truly professional manager, however, knows that a sound
solution is the result of the systematic application of mental effort,
and that the *process* of developing such a solution can be studied
and learned just like any other skill.

Whether we are solving a problem ourselves or helping someone
else solve a problem, the best place to begin is with a good practical
understanding of the problem-solving process.

> 'A problem is a gap between the ideal or the goal and the actual
> state of affairs. You begin by gathering data and defining the
> problem clearly. Then and only then do you start looking at
> solution options. You survey a full range of options, using a bit
> of creative brainstorming if need be, before trying to zero in on
> a single option...'

This is the sort of basic stuff that a model has to contain. It has to be
simple, with no more than five or six steps. It has to be couched in very
plain and practical terms. And, once you have it, you have to stick with
it until it becomes a natural part of the way you look at things.

There are a lot of different models of the problem-solving process.
They all represent the logical sequence of questions we should ask in

trying to arrive at an answer to the big question: 'What am I going to do?'. The critical thing isn't that you have the right model. There is no such thing; one is about as good as another. The critical thing is that you have a model in your mind and that you stick with it so that it becomes an ingrained, integral part of the way you look at things.

> **You have to have a logical, step-by-step model that suits you – and you have to use it consistently.**

Even a simple model, ingrained in one's mind and used instinctively, is better than a much more elaborate or conceptually accurate model that is too complex or too obtuse to understand and use.

There are two important guidelines that we should probably keep in mind as we proceed. First, keep it simple. Second, keep it natural.

Keeping things as simple as possible

The number **seven** is important. Seven, plus or minus two, is reportedly the number of things that a human being can keep in his or her head – actively – at any one time. So it's a good idea to never sketch out a list or a flowchart or a diagram, if it's something you have to remember or learn to use *intuitively*, with more than seven steps in it.

And our problem-solving model is, most definitely and most emphatically, something that we want to remember and learn to use intuitively.

Keeping things as 'natural' as possible

We don't want to stray too far from the way you think about and solve problems right now. You might, for example, view the problem-solving process as consisting of two simple steps:

- I think about the problem, and then...
- I decide what to do.

This might raise some questions. For example, what caused you to think about the problem in the first place? Did someone bring it to your attention? Was it dumped in your lap? Is it just something that happened?

Another question might be raised about the deciding-what-to-do part of your model. *Doing things* isn't all that simple. It may require getting the time and commitment of other people. People with pressures and problems and priorities of their own. It may involve a complex sequence of action steps. It may involve spending money, or changing the way people do things, or getting the powers that be to re-think a long-standing corporate policy.

So our two-step model might better reflect the reality of things by being expanded a bit:

- A problem comes to my attention.
- I think about the problem, and then . . .
- I decide what to do.
- Then I do it.

It shouldn't take too much convincing to add on a couple more steps:

- A problem comes to my attention.
- I investigate, ask a few questions, get the facts.
- I think about the problem, and then . . .
- I decide what to do.
- I then do it.
- Then I look at the results to see if the problem has been solved.

The last step – looking at the results – is a useful one because it's like the snake eating its tail. It's the step that feeds back into the beginning of the process. As you look at the results of your problem-solving action, you go back to the beginning of the cycle if the problem still hasn't gone away. You start over again, hopefully with the problem at least partially solved. Either way, you have a new problem to solve and you have to start the process all over again.

USING A SIX-STEP MODEL

Let's go with the **six-step model** depicted in Figure 1. We've broken the thinking-about-the-problem step into *two* steps – Step Three, where we define the problem, and Step Four, where we scan or generate an array of possible solutions. And we've left off the

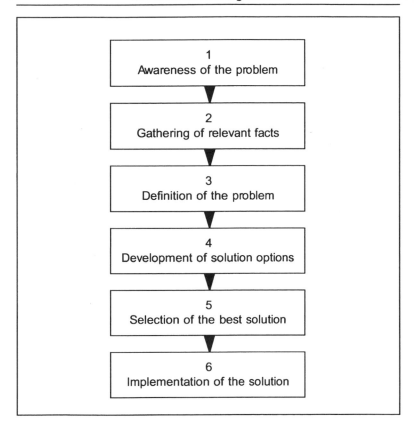

Fig. 1. The six step problem-solving model.

closing-of-the-loop portion. We'll treat that as a recycling of the process rather than as a separate 'step' therein.

Our model, then, contains six separate steps. The first three steps have to do with defining the problem. The next three steps move us from the understanding phase into the solution phase: exploring and developing a variety of solution options and then acting upon the best one.

Before discussing the various steps of the model in detail we need to clearly understand that this is just a model – not reality. In actual practice, the steps in the model do not follow one after the other in a definite and orderly fashion. Deliberations at one step in the sequence may cause us to go back and reconsider or recycle a previous step. Some problems or decisions may not require that a

lot of time be devoted to this or that specific step, or the pressures of
time may not allow it.

> **In practice, there is considerable overlap amongst the six steps,
> and a good deal of skipping back and forth.**

So let's treat the model as a convenient checklist of basic steps
needed to bring order to the problem-solving and decision-making
process. And it is, as we have already agreed, an *iterative* model where
Step Six connects back into Step One and re-starts the whole cycle.

PROBLEM-SOLVING VERSUS DECISION-MAKING

We should probably clarify these terms, and now is a good time to
do so – before we get too far into our discussion.

We've said that a problem is a gap between the way things are and
the way they ought to be.

A decision, on the other hand, is a choice between two or more
alternatives. It may involve a crisp yes-or-no answer or it may mean
choosing the best from a set of alternatives which are all satisfactory.
So, decision-making is really a sub-set of problem-solving.

It can also be argued that decision-making is actually a much
broader concept. Where 'problem-solving' concerns itself with
things that have already happened and is largely done by people on
the lower rungs of the organisational ladder, decision-making
focuses on building and shaping the future and is the province of
managers at the more senior levels of the hierarchy (Figure 2).

Problem-solving is:	Decision-making is:
• focused on the past	• focused on the future
• usually analytical	• often creative
• operational	• directional
• done at lower levels.	• done at senior levels.

Fig. 2. Problem-solving and decision-making.

The boundary line between problem-solving and decision-making is also made rather fuzzy by the fact that having to *make* a decision can be a problem. My daughter has to decide between going on a three-day trip to Ross-on-Wye with her school class, which would mean missing her weekend choir practice (with an important concert looming on the horizon), or going to the choir practice but foregoing the school trip.

A few more examples:

- It comes down to Mike and Ruth. Both excellent candidates. Who gets the job?

- The fact that the product did well in the States doesn't mean that it will sell in the UK. Do we go with it?

- Do we start at the top and work down, or is this one of those situations where we use the end-run strategy?

We'll largely ignore this category of problem from here on in. Let's just recognise that when we give Jack or Judy a tough decision to make, what we're effectively saying is – *It's your problem, Jack or Judy; you deal with it.*

MUDDLING THROUGH

Question – *Does the model that we are developing in this chapter reflect how managers actually solve problems...or how they* could *if they put their minds to it?* If it does, then that's fine. If it doesn't, then when we try to put the model into practice, we're quite likely to be disappointed with the results that we get.

Most managers would probably lay out a four- or five- or six-step model not unlike the one we are developing here. The exact definition of steps would vary from manager or manager, but the core process would undoubtedly be there.

It's difficult to know, however, whether that means that this is actually how managers go about solving the problems they face on a day-to-day basis. It might be that is simply the way they feel they *ought* to go about it.

Considering the implications

Let's go back to our question. Does our step-by-step problem-solving model stand up in practice?

By and large, it doesn't. In reality, managers don't make much use of a formal model. Their *staff* might. The people who write their briefing papers might sing the praises of a formal model and swear that everyone should use it. But not the practising manager. At least... not consciously.

> **Managers don't make much use of a formal, step-by-step model of the problem-solving process.**

There in the background
Let's not throw the baby out with the bathwater. Just because the buzz of activity that we see on the surface bears little relation to our formal, step-by-step model there is no reason to throw it out entirely.

> **Having a model of the problem-solving process, if it does nothing else, gives us a goal to aim for.**

It also gives us a frame of reference, a common language, in our discussions with colleagues and subordinates.

And, most importantly, it's there in the background, guiding our thinking, even when we are not conscious of its playing an active role.

Facing the challenge
The challenge we face, in becoming more effective as problem-solvers and decision-makers, is that of *starting* with a stepwise model of the fundamental process, recognising its limitations, and using it effectively. Using it effectively in the sense of adapting it to the realities of the environment, keeping it in the background *consciously* rather than unconsciously, knowing precisely where and when and how and why it has to be adapted as we use it in practice.

KEY POINTS

- A problem is basically a deviation from the norm, serious enough to require correction. Something is not the way it should be.

- Problem-solving is the process we use to bring these two elements back into alignment. It's how we close the gap.

- Problem-solving is something that a lot of us take for granted.

- The truly professional manager, however, knows that problem-solving can be studied and learned just like any other skill.

- The best place to begin is with a simple, easy-to-understand, step-by-step model of the problem-solving process.

- The critical thing is that you have a model you stick with so that it becomes an ingrained, integral part of the way you look at things.

- Our model contains six separate steps which find their way into most problem-solving situations.

- In actual practice, there is considerable overlap amongst the six steps, and a good deal of skipping back and forth.

- The model is an iterative one which means that Step Six connects back into Step One and re-starts the whole cycle.

- In reality, managers don't make much use of a formal, step-by-step model of the problem-solving process.

- Still, having a model of the problem-solving process gives us a goal to aim for. It serves as a useful warning to go one step at a time.

- Our challenge in becoming more effective problem-solvers is to recognise the model's limitations and use it effectively irregardless.

2
Becoming Aware of the Problem

The first step in the problem-solving process is to become aware of the problem – to recognise that something isn't the way it should be. We sense that something is amiss. Things aren't happening quite the way we want them to happen.

In Figure 3 we ask ourselves four simple questions.

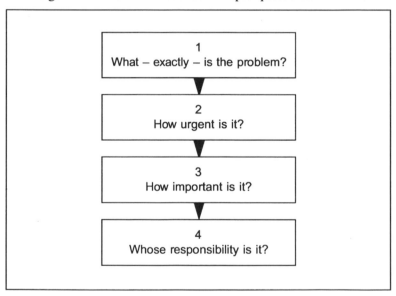

Fig. 3. Becoming aware of the problem.

ASKING FOUR SIMPLE QUESTIONS

1. What exactly is the problem?
Okay, we've just lost the Hollander account. That's the problem we're faced with. There's a good degree of urgency associated with it, because it's an important account.

The first thing we have to do is ascertain exactly what has happened.

- Laura Riggins, their buyer, is hopping mad and is threatening to cancel their business with us.

- Laura said something that seemed to *imply* that she was going to cancel their business with us.

- She has just signed a two-year contract with one of our chief competitors, effectively shutting us out.

- Frances, Laura's boss and the category manager, has opted to go with the competition.

- Frank has really screwed something up badly and is afraid that we might end up losing the Hollander business.

None of these five things constitute *good* news, but they are not all equally bad – and they have different connotations in regard to the action we might wish to take at this stage. So it is important to know exactly what we are dealing with.

2. How urgent is it?

How urgent is the problem? Is it urgent enough that I should clear the decks and give it absolute top priority or can it wait until tomorrow?

Some problems *are* urgent. Let's acknowledge that. If you're responsible for getting baked goods into your customer's 325 stores across the UK, and there's a store manager in Leeds whose delivery is a half-hour late or has got the quantities all wrong, then you have to move quickly. This is a stop-the-bleeding situation. The key thing now is to do whatever is needed to solve the customer's immediate problem.

But such problems are very much the exception rather than the rule. Or they ought to be. If crisis management is the order of the day in your job, then that in itself is a problem that has to be addressed.

3. How important is it?

Urgent problems clamour for attention but that doesn't necessarily reflect their importance in the overall scheme of things. Fixing a flat tyre on your car is urgent. You can't drive unless you do it. Getting your oil changed regularly, though hardly urgent, is very important in terms of safeguarding your car's health and welfare over the long haul.

> **The point is this. We can't afford to allow *urgency* alone to govern our response to problems. The *importance* factor has to be entered into the equation as well.**

That's a logical statement, and a good idea. But when and how would we actually 'address' the problem? Would it mean closing the office door and asking our PA to hold all our calls and then sitting there at the desk and *thinking* about the issue?

And then, of course, the real question. *Will we actually do it?*

4. Whose responsibility is it?

Whose problem is it? No – that's not the right way to phrase things. It's *our* problem. Whose *responsibility* is it? That's better.

Back to crisis management. The urgent problem is the store in Leeds. The underlying problem is the fact that there is a store in Leeds costing you £££s every day of the week. It's eating away at your time. And, most crucially, it's preventing you from playing the sort of strategic planning cum business management role which your boss says that you *should* be playing in relation to this important national account.

Clearly, problem-solving at both levels is your responsibility. Resolving to close the door and *think* about the issue is futile, because we both know that that isn't going to happen. A decision to think about the issue while you're driving along the M25 or the M1 is more likely to be acted upon, but how *effective* is your thinking likely to be while you're trying to keep an eye on the traffic at the same time?

But the more important point is that addressing the issue may not even be something that you should be doing all by yourself. It makes much more sense, in this specific case, to have lunch with the customer's baked goods buyer or category manager. See whether the two of you can work out a solution that could be carried further through the creation of an *ad hoc* group involving people from both sides. And you might want, before you have that lunch, to consult with someone to see whether they can come up with some ideas for putting a solution in place.

> **The important thing is that the problem be addressed by the right people at the right time – and that you be responsible for activating and managing the process.**

The point is this. Yes, you're responsible for seeing that the problem is dealt with. But no, you don't have to deal with it yourself. Not directly. You can stand back and manage the **process** which enables the problem to be solved effectively.

OUR FIRST REACTION – THE PITFALLS

Let's talk again about how we react to a problem when it first presents itself. There are three thoughts which are quite likely to pass through our mind:

- This is a problem.
- I've got to solve it.
- I'd better do something.

We shouldn't take these assumptions at face value and we certainly shouldn't *act* upon them. If we do, then we fall into one of the four major pitfalls which await the unwary problem-solver at this first stage in the problem-solving process.

1. Jumping too quickly into action

The first question we generally ask ourselves when we discover a problem is *What do I do?* or *What do we do?* There's nothing wrong with that – as long as we don't answer it right away. We want to take action in a way that solves the problem.

When we first see a problem it may seem quite straightforward. And, in our eagerness to come to grips with the situation it is very tempting to plunge ahead.

But – nine times out of ten, if we just take action or bark out an order, right then and there, we'll be wrong. At some point, usually after considerable effort has been expended, we'll discover that we have been nibbling away ineffectually at the fringes of the real problem or perhaps even working on the wrong problem altogether.

In all but the simplest problem situations, there is no obvious right action to take. If there was, the situation would hardly warrant being called a 'problem', and it certainly shouldn't have been brought to our attention whether we call it a 'problem' or not. Someone else should have handled it. Routinely.

Pitfall Number 1: Jumping too quickly into action
One of the biggest and most common mistakes that people make

when faced with a problem is that of jumping too quickly into action.

It is commonly assumed that successful managers make *quick* decisions. But even just a day or two working with a successful manager will show that such is not the case. Good managers don't make snap judgements. They take as much time as they need to find out what sort of situation they are dealing with and they seldom make a decision before the time for action arrives.

After all, why make a decision before it is actually needed? In a fluid situation especially, it makes much more sense to get to work *thinking* about a problem and gathering information about it – but not deciding what action to take until it is time to act. That way, our decision is made in *real time*, on the basis of the latest and most accurate intelligence.

Pitfall Number One, then, involves jumping too quickly into action. Only rarely – in a crisis situation – will a decision need to be made that quickly. And, if that happens, your second action should be to sit down and figure out why the crisis occurred in the first place and how it can be prevented from occurring again.

2. Treating symptoms rather than causes

All too often managers make decisions without having clearly defined the problem they are trying to solve. They take the apparent problem as the problem and then focus quickly on trying to figure out what to do about it. In other words, they skip Step Two – the gathering of relevant facts – and Step Three – the definition of the problem.

How do we avoid the danger of treating symptoms rather than tackling the basic problem? The best way is to proceed the way a good physician proceeds when a patient complains of headaches, nausea, etc. A good physician treats these symptoms – and then proceeds to question and probe ... searching for facts, until they can say with a high degree of certainty that the 'problem' has been pinned down. Once that has been done, the solution is usually obvious.

That's the way we have to proceed. In the interests of being sure that we end up tackling the real problem, we have to treat our initial identification of the problem as a hypothesis to be tested out. To test it out, we have to stop and gather the facts that will allow us to identify the core problem.

Assume that what you're seeing is merely a signal – a sign that a problem exists.

3. Assuming that you have to solve it

Don't assume that the problem is *yours* to solve. More often than not, it won't be.

> **If you are a manager, especially, your role is more that of a problem *discoverer* than a problem *solver*. That's where you add your value and make your vital contribution.**

There are a number of ways in which the value you add is unique. More than the people working under your wings, for example, you are in a position to take the overview on a key issue – to see the big picture.

Even if you're *not* a manager that still doesn't mean that you have to solve every problem that you come across. Sometimes, you can make a much more important contribution by *identifying who should tackle the problem*.

It means thinking like a chief executive officer or managing director. And what the latter does is ask themselves a simple question: *Who's the person in this organisation best equipped or best positioned to solve this problem?* Is this a problem that I should be dealing with? Would I be better to spend a half-hour briefing Harriet and turning the whole situation over to her? Should I stay involved in the situation but see if I can't get Bill or Charlie to do the legwork?

As a rule, most of us – unless we're senior managers – are reluctant to assign problems to other people over whom we have no authority. Who are *we*, after all, to tell Harriet that we've decided that she is the person in this organisation best equipped or best positioned to solve this problem?

Pitfall Number 3: Assuming that you have to solve it
One of the most common *myths* about management is that the main function of the manager is to make decisions. The fact of the matter is that good managers don't make a lot of decisions. They *manage* decision-making and decision-makers.

Twenty or thirty years ago, perhaps, a manager could get away with pulling in the reins and making all the major decisions. These days, managers seldom know enough about the jobs being done under their jurisdiction to step in and start making decisions about day-to-day technical matters. And most of us recognise that stepping in and making decisions about non-technical matters is both a waste of valuable managerial time and a real demotivator for the people under us.

Good managers don't do it. They stick to managing the decision-making **process**. They stand by to run interference, liaise at the senior levels, or get people the resources they need. And, perhaps most importantly of all, they assign a high priority to developing their people's skills and confidence as problem-solvers and decision-makers.

Case study

One of our *Famous Five* – Graeme Weir – answered the question this way:

> 'I want my people to be thinking like mini-CEO's. It really bothers me when I see someone wasting a whole afternoon struggling with a problem that they are not equipped to handle. Why not make an executive decision – show some initiative – and pass the problem along to the right person? That's what I want my people to be doing. Thinking, and acting, like executives rather than junior supervisors.'

Why not? It sounds straightforward enough. But, for the average corporation, such a simple idea represents an enormous turnaround in the way we think about things.

4. Assuming it's good to be problem-free

What would it be like to work in a hassle-free, problem-free environment – where everyone is well motivated, competent and superbly trained, where your customers are happy and your shareholders are content and your share of the market is downright sinful..?

Worrisome.

Life shouldn't be like that. And on those rare days when it *seems* that way, you should very quickly set about creating a disturbance of some sort. To create the demand for something a bit more innovative and a bit more daring than what we did yesterday.

The point we're making is that one of the manager's most crucial roles is that of **tension-creator**. No one has said it better than Murray Lincoln, the well-known co-operative leader on the American side of the Atlantic:

'Any organisation, once it becomes successful, is apt to lose its original drive and vision. Because this is so, I've often suggested that we have a vice-president in charge of revolution. He'd be one man not responsible for any operations. He'd stand to one side, with whatever staff he needed, to pick holes in whatever we were doing and remind us of our basic philosophy, our fundamental concepts. His job would be to stir up everything and everybody, to criticise and challenge everything being done – objectives, methods, programmes, results. Executives get into ruts...I would want my vice-president in charge of revolution to spend time throwing us off balance, shaking us out of our coziness, making us feel a little insecure and uncertain.'

THE 'OH SH-T' PROBLEM

We have been implying all along that some problems are *urgent* and have to be dealt with as such.

- I'm going to be late for the meeting.
- I'm going to have to skip the meeting altogether.
- The report didn't go out as promised.
- They didn't get the report.

We've used the term **crisis management**. The 'Oh Sh-t' label is a term which somewhat more accurately captures how problems of this ilk are described by practising managers. And this is what a lot of people think of when they think of 'problem'.

Such problems, we agreed, should be the exception rather than the rule. Be that as it may, let's talk briefly about how to deal with them.

First of all, accept what has happened. Calmly and objectively. don't fret about what you can't change. The deadline is here and the report isn't done. And – sadly – the people you thought you could count on just aren't there when you need them.

Don't waste time fretting over what has happened and can't be changed. Focus all your attention on what has to happen *now* – and an hour from now, and tomorrow, and the day after – in order to make the best of a bad situation.

The only time you look backwards is when you need information. What, for example, do we mean when we say that the project has been sidetracked? Let's be precise about it so that we know what we're dealing with.

And then visualise a successful conclusion to the whole sordid affair. Okay, then – the people on the receiving end, be it a customer or otherwise – aren't happy with what happened, but at least they feel that you handled it professionally and salvaged what you could for them. If anything, you've won points for your diligence in responding promptly to an unfortunate turn of events – and for honestly and truly giving their needs top priority.

And then, figure out how you achieved that positive outcome. Work backwards. What exactly did you do that led to the reasonably palatable state of affairs which we have just described? Who did you call or talk to? What, exactly, were the words that you used – and in what tone of voice were they delivered? What actions were taken, and who exactly was involved in taking them?

Finally, make it happen. Get started. The sooner the better.

KEEPING YOUR ANTENNA UP

One of your biggest challenges as a manager is to avoid getting so busy, so tied up with specific meetings and activities and the like, that you stop having time for just getting out there and sniffing around to see what's happening.

Getting out there and walking around

You're not going to become aware of a problem if you're wading through a stack of papers from your in-tray or diligently reading your way through a thirty-page report. You might become aware of certain specific problems described in the report, and various items from your in-tray may be useful in bringing specific issues to your attention. But these things are rarely urgent. By and large, if they have to do with problems at all, they have to do with problems which have already been acted upon or at least identified and allocated to someone for handling.

No, to become *aware* of problems you have to be out there where things are happening, not stuck in your office.

> **Good managers make it a practice to do a lot of what most of us have learned to call 'managing by walking around'.**

Good managers recognise the importance of getting out there and just 'circulating', and they make time for it.

Taking samples

When you pop your head into Jim Pascoe's office and ask him how the revision of the divisional marketing plan is coming along, he's probably going to tell you that it's coming along quite well, thank you very much. Or that there have been a couple of dodgy points but that everything is under control. He's unlikely to give you much more than the most general of overviews because you are, after all, 'managing by walking around' and he doesn't want to take up too much of your time or bore you with a lot of details. Plus, he doesn't want to appear to be a 'details man'.

Still, it wouldn't hurt to probe for some specific details on one or two key points. High-level executives often do this as a way of *sampling* the person's thinking. If the person can give you a lucid, coherent, well-thought-through response to just one or two tough, probing, sharp-edged questions, then you can walk away with the assurance that things are well under control.

Staying close to the customer

It is especially important that you stay close to the customer. The reason is simple. It is better to become aware of a problem by hearing through the grapevine that your customer has been talking to the competition than by seeing – two months later – a sudden drop in the amount of product being sold into that account. In the first instance, you have time to do something to maintain your edge. In the second, it's too late.

The lunch in the caféteria with your opposite number in that other department, your attendance at the monthly trade meeting, your half-hour chat on the telephone with one of your major customers, your taking time out from a busy schedule to investigate something which you *know* is going to make an important customer unhappy...these are all wise investments of your time. They allow you to keep in touch with what's happening, and to spot issues and discomforts before they can blossom into full-blown problems. If a problem *does* occur, they allow you to understand much more quickly and astutely what the real problem is, why it has occurred, and what has to be done about it.

Trusting your instincts

Problems sometimes come to our attention in very tenuous, ill-defined form.

For some people, this lack of precision doesn't present a problem. They take pride in having a good 'feel' for things and have learned to trust that feel when the time comes to identify something as a problem or to make a decision.

For other people, however, the idea of moving ahead on the basis of something as tenuous as one's *feel* for things or one's *instinct* in regard to a situation would be uncomfortable if not totally unthinkable.

And it's not just accountants and engineers who think that way. It has long been recognised that the way people think tends to lean distinctly toward one of two poles. There's a linear, sequential, logical, analytical mode of thinking that is supposedly related to the **left** hemisphere of the human brain and is called **left-brain** thinking. And there is a holistic, relational, non-linear way of thinking which is associated with the brain's **right** hemisphere and is therefore referred to as **right-brain** thinking. Although it's difficult to be terribly exact about these things, if you stopped a hundred commuters at Charing Cross station and gave them each a brief test of left-versus-right-brain dominance, you would probably find that you had about an equal number of each.

If you're a left-brain sort of person, you'll have to make a special effort to learn to trust or at least pay attention to your instincts. A dog can *sense* that its owner is about to arrive home quite a bit before a human can hear the sound of a car in the driveway. And a good manager can *sense* that something is awry long before the average manager reads about it in the form of a worrisome dip in a vital statistic or ratio.

Whether we can actually develop our instincts is debatable. What we *can* do is recognise their importance as a monitoring device and pay attention when they make their presence felt.

Looking in the mirror

The problem that we are *least* likely to be aware of is the one that involves *us* – as a manager. The one that stems from the way we do things, or the way we handled a specific situation or dealt with a specific individual.

- We're overbearing.

- We put people off.

- We're too quick to jump in and do people's thinking for them.

- We get impatient with people.

- We seem reluctant to come right out and tell people what to do.

- We spend too much time behind closed doors.

Coming to terms with the truth about ourselves is difficult. Think, for example, of how it feels when you hear your voice on a tape recording or video. Hearing how we actually *sound* to other people can be quite disheartening.

If you are in a position to influence how your company trains its managers, what you want to do is push for the use of real, live feedback on real, live behaviour. That's how people learn best. Whether it's a matter of learning to swim or learning to manage, you can only learn so much by reading a book or having someone stand at the front of a conference room and *talk* about it.

The suggestion here is that you create such learning experiences for yourself.

Case study
Jack Carter, one of our *Famous Five* put it this way:

'I've been in discussion groups – they used to call them T-Groups – where people are supposed to "open up" with one another, usually with the help of a moderator and some special exercises. The idea's okay, but the whole thing left a sour taste in people's mouths. A couple of years ago, I started using 360° feedback, just within my own team of people. What it does is give me some hard data on how I actually behave as a manager, and what impact that has on people. And that, believe me, is powerful.'

When and wherever possible – routinise
Imagine we had a package that was due to be mailed, which *had* to be in the recipient's hands by tomorrow, and which wasn't quite ready for the afternoon post. The first time it happened, we had a *bona fide* problem-solving situation on our hands. We had to think about alternate ways of getting the package delivered and figure out which one would work best. The second and third time it happened, on the other hand, we knew what to do. We didn't have to think about it.

The idea here is to **routinise** problems when and wherever we can. Routinising may be as simple as making a mental note of what we did. Or, at the other end of the scale, it might mean writing up a procedure and pasting it into the operations manual. Somewhere between these two extremes, we might find ourselves putting a note on Shirley's desk or advising through simple word-of-mouth how problems should be dealt with.

> **Every time we routinise something, it's one less problem to solve.**
> **One less decision to make. One less thing to think about.**

The benefits of doing so should be obvious. Every time we routinise something, it's one less problem to solve.

Putting controls in place
This is one specific way of routinising a problem – putting some control in place so that you know when something needs to be attended to *before* it becomes a problem. If our profit projections for April are out of line because of an unexpected increase in administrative costs then let's put something in place that warns us in advance when this is going to happen.

If you don't have a problem, find one!
If it ain't broke, break it! The idea is basically the same. If things seem a bit too quiet then what you might want to do is to assume that disaster lies just around the corner. The competition is just about to come out with something that even your most loyal customers will find irresistible.

So this is no time to be complacent. How can we do things better to make the best product on the market even better?

In other words, if you don't *have* a problem to solve, *create* one.

KEY POINTS

- Avoid jumping in with both feet every time something untoward happens. Not every symptom heralds a problem requiring active attention.

- Treat red flags as symptoms rather than causes until further investigation has been done. Proceed the way a good physician would.

- Treat a crisis like a crisis. Move quickly, confidently, and authoritatively in those situations where decisive action is required.

- Focus on delegating rather than doing in those situations where someone else could or should deal with the problem.

- Get out there and walk around, with the explicit purpose of sniffing out potential problems before they become problems.

- Trust your instincts – not totally, but certainly enough that you pay attention and investigate further when they suggest a problem.

- Develop controls which shift problems from one-off crises to deviation-type problems with routine solutions.

- Cultivate specific people and vehicles best positioned to alert you to potential problems before they become problems.

- Become aware of the difference between proactive and reactive problem-solving. Try to do more of the former and less of the latter.

3
Gathering the Relevant Facts

Before we decide what to do, before we even say that we know for sure what the real problem is . . . we have to go through the discipline of **gathering the facts**. And it *does* involve discipline. It is so tempting to skimp a bit at this stage in the problem-solving cycle. To get on with the 'managerial' tasks of coming out with a statement of what the problem is, or putting a bold and forward-looking plan into effect. But gathering facts? That almost sounds as if we're not *doing* anything about the problem.

GETTING GOOD INFORMATION

Rarely will we have time to get all the information we need. Still – to understand the problem, we need at the very least to collect and analyse the **critical** facts relevant to the situation. Indeed, it's not enough just to gather them. We have to understand what they mean.

We have to be focused
It is important that we never forget *why* we are searching for information, and what that information has to do for us.

- In the case of a **Fix-It** problem, our goal is to find out what is *causing* the problem.

- In the case of a **Do-It** problem, our goal is to clarify where we want to end up and where we are starting from.

We have to keep our goal clearly in mind and we don't stop gathering information until it has been achieved. But, when it has been achieved, we stop.

We have to be selective
Fact-finding has to be a sharply focused effort. We need to know in advance what information is going to be essential and what is not.

Otherwise, we may end up moving ahead on the basis of a large array of facts and yet have relatively little information on the most significant aspects of the problem.

Case study

Jennifer Adair, Customer Service Manager with a London-based tour operator and one of our *Famous Five*, described the reality of how this is done:

'I sniff around for information, usually by talking informally with people – in their office, over lunch, before or after a meeting – and then perhaps raising the issue briefly during a team meeting. At this stage, I don't need all the details. What I want to understand is how people are being affected. How is the problem interfering with their getting things done? Is there an impact on the delivery of service? At a later stage, once we've put a task force together or I've given someone the job of taking things further, we can worry about the details. At this stage, it's the overview that I'm after. The outcomes.'

The outcomes
We've talked before about the fact that our six-step model of the problem-solving process is – like all good models – a useful simplification. And what should be guiding our information-gathering efforts at Step Two is a knowledge of how we will want to *define* the problem when we get to Step Three – what parameters will be involved.

> **The template used to define the problem at Step Three will govern the information we need to gather at Step Two.**

Looking for meaning

We have to figure out what the facts mean. We have to analyse their significance in relation to the problem we are trying to solve. So we have to extrapolate. The facts alone, as they are, have little or nothing to tell us.

Case study

Back to Jennifer:

'Is this a one-off problem or a systems problem? That's one of the first questions I ask myself. If it's a one-off problem, and the person involved hasn't been able to solve it, then often all I have to do is give him or her a little nudge in the right direction or nod my approval for something they want to do. But if it's what I call a "systems" problem – something that has to do with how we deal with a whole class of customer-related problems – then I'll get a lot more involved because we're looking at something which will probably have a bearing on how the team as a whole operates.'

ASKING THE RIGHT QUESTIONS

As is true of so many other things, fact-finding is largely a matter of asking ourselves the right questions. Lists of such questions are often supplied by textbooks on problem-solving and decision-making, but the questions included are, of necessity, quite general. More to the point, a checklist shouldn't be needed once you've recognised the importance and purpose of asking questions in the first place and got into a proper inquiring frame of mind.

- *What* has happened, and precisely *how* did it happen? In the interests of objectivity, we want to make sure that we examine the situation from every viewpoint and arrive at an assessment that everyone involved can concur with.

- *Where* and *when* did the problem occur? Is the location factor or the time factor of significance?

- *Who* are the people involved in the situation, and in what way does, or did, their involvement affect the situation? Can we expect their behaviour to change in any way?

- *Why* hasn't the situation resolved itself? Surely someone would have looked into it by now and sorted things out. Is there something here that I'm missing?

Notice the magic words. **What, who, why, where, when.** These are good words to be using, because they're inquisitive words. They're the words of someone who's looking for an answer and hasn't found it yet.

One question should lead to another. It's a sign that you're digging, that your questions – or, more precisely, the *answers* you get – are leading you somewhere.

GETTING OUT AND TALKING TO PEOPLE

The above section underscores the importance of asking questions, but it needn't imply that you yourself have to supply all the answers. In most situations, the best way to gather information about a problem is to get out there and talk to the people involved.

- So what's happening, Jim?
- When did you first notice something was wrong?
- Any idea which direction it came from?
- What do you think would happen if we removed it?
- Has all this had any effect on the work you do?
- How do things look from where you sit, Karen?
- Any idea what we should be doing about all this?
- Anything I've missed?

What we're doing here is systematically collecting individual opinions and viewpoints. That means we should decide in advance who to talk to and what specific ground to cover with our queries.

> **It is generally good to solicit some individual opinions and observations before going after the same information using a *group* format.**

Once people gather together around a conference table, there are usually two or three members of the team who become less forthcoming or candid than they would be in a one-to-one situation.

TAPPING OTHER SOURCES

What we do after talking to people will depend on the sort of information we need to gather, and that will depend in turn on the sort of problem we are dealing with.

If sales of one of our products has been sluggish, we'll need some data to tell us just how badly things have fallen off and where exactly that has happened. That sort of information should be on the computer somewhere. If it can't be printed out at the press of a key or two, find someone who can extract precisely the information you need in the form that you need it.

If the introduction of a new inventory control system is two months behind schedule, then talking to people will probably be our main information-gathering strategy. But we'll also want to look at whatever project management or project-related data is available – just to see what has been done. After talking to people, here are just a few of the other things we can do...

- Get out Bill's report and read it.

- Call a meeting of the whole team.

- Have lunch with the customer.

- Stop in at the library.

- Call the industry association.

- Ask accounting to print out last quarter's results.

- Download some data from the computer.

There is also a whole host of information and data available through the company library, the local public library, the Internet, various industry associations, and various governmental or agency bodies. Too *much* information, in some cases, underscores the need to be selective and to remain keenly aware of the passage of time.

Let's note, incidentally, that we are talking primarily about **Fix-It** problems at this stage. **Do-It** problems also involve the gathering of information but of a slightly different sort. We'll come back to this point shortly.

REPRESENTING THE FACTS

The idea of **representing** refers to capturing the facts in statistical form or even just writing them down. The key is getting them on paper where we can see them succinctly, at a glance. This is especially important when the problem is a complex or multi-faceted one, where it is difficult to hold all the information about it in our mind at one time and think about it coherently. And yet it is in regard to just this sort of problem that we need to be able to stand back and look at things holistically.

> **Your mind should be reserved for *thinking*,
> not used as a storage house.**

DOING A FORCE-FIELD ANALYSIS

The idea of doing a **force-field analysis** originated many years ago. It's a simple but very useful way of looking at the dynamics of a problem situation. What it does is show, in graphic form, the forces working for and against a particular state of affairs. It is assumed that, in a given situation, the status quo is an **equilibrium** which is being maintained by a combination of forces – some pushing the equilibrium toward a goal or objective and others, the restraining or opposing forces, resisting that push.

Figure 4 illustrates the basics. There are two forces acting on the situation, shown in Figure 4 – the pressure to decide and the uncertainty about what to do. The pressure and the uncertainty are acting in equal – let's make them both 2 on a scale of 1 (mild) to 3 (high) – but opposite directions to bring the whole problem-solving process to a halt.

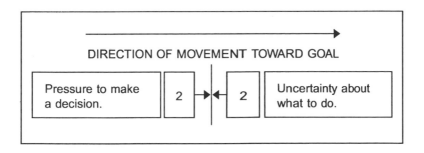

DIRECTION OF MOVEMENT TOWARD GOAL

| Pressure to make a decision. | 2 | | 2 | Uncertainty about what to do. |

Fig. 4. Force-field analysis.

To change things, to allow the equilibrium to move to the right, we have two choices. First, we can up the pressure. *For God's sake, don't just stand there – make a decision!*

Second, we can reduce the force on the right, the restraining or oppositional force – the uncertainty about what to do. We can do that by providing a rule to follow. This first time around, we'll give verbal instructions – after that, we'll write it into the operations manual so that similar situations can be handled quite routinely in future. The rule might be something like this:

- If re-scheduling means that shipping has to break up a full truck load, don't do it. Otherwise, re-schedule. Or...

- Speak to your assistant, Sam. Sam's been here 17 years and he knows all about these things. Or...

- Ask the paint shop supervisor what he thinks ought to be done and then tell him to go ahead and do it.

The beauty of this analysis is that it forces us to recognise that the way things are is the result of a number of different forces acting to produce a temporary equilibrium – and that *reducing* the forces working against what we want to achieve is just as valid as increasing the forces that are moving us toward the goal. Let's look at a more detailed example.

CASE STUDY

Quitting smoking

Let's get away from the business world for a minute and assume that our problem is that of quitting smoking. Specifically, we smoke and we don't want to. So it's a problem.

Let's subject the problem to a force-field analysis. It means drawing a diagram (Figure 5). On the left side we'll draw arrows representing all the things that are pushing us toward the goal of quitting smoking.

On the right side of the diagram, we draw an arrow for each of the things that is preventing us from quitting.

As a strategy to quit smoking, there are a number of things we can do. The pressure to quit that stems from the *cost* of smoking. The lack of a *need* to quit today can be sharply reduced if our doctor announces that we're now a high-risk candidate for a stroke or heart attack.

In short, there are a lot of ways to move the equilibrium toward the right-hand side of the diagram. And the good thing about using a force-field analysis is that it helps us identify a wider array of strategies than we might otherwise examine.

Including feelings

Feelings often need to be included in our fact-gathering. In the

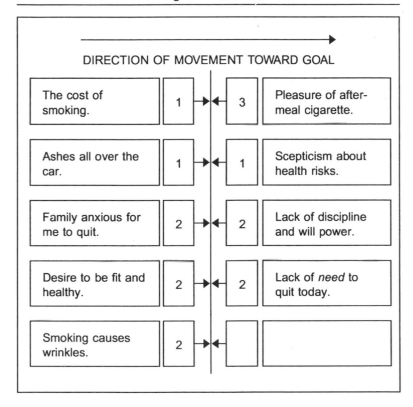

Fig. 5. Force-field analysis 2.

force-field analysis we just did in the quitting-smoking problem we should have added one more item to our list of forces pushing us toward quitting. I'm *tired* of smoking. I don't *want* to be a smoker any more.

That's probably the best reason of all for quitting. I just *want* to do it. I want to be the sort of person who doesn't smoke. So we enter it as an arrow in our force-field diagram. A *big* arrow, because it's an important factor. And when we do that, the whole balance of the diagram shifts.

EXAMINING OTHER TECHNIQUES

There are quite a few different ways to capture information on paper or on the computer screen, and we are going to look at some of them here. But we'll do so briefly.

> **Choose a way to represent information that acts *effectively* to help you see things in perspective.**

The key point is that *how* you lay information out is very important. You have to choose a method that is appropriate to the sort of information you are gathering – and 'appropriate' means that it acts *effectively* to help you keep the information in perspective and develop a sense of how the data you have gathered all adds up.

SWOT analysis
Strengths, Weaknesses, Opportunities, Threats – that's what the letters SWOT stand for. Figure 6 provides four boxes into which the information and ideas and opinions we collect can be channelled.

Like any other collected of 'boxes', it plays a helpful role by simply forcing us to put something into each of the four boxes. What are the threats we have to worry about? We know what our strengths are; how about our weaknesses? The model works its magic, in other words, by simply posing the questions.

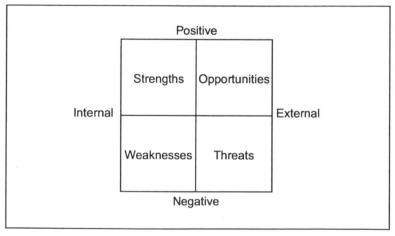

Fig. 6. SWOT analysis.

Pareto charts
A **Pareto chart** is a special form of vertical bar chart designed to direct our attention away from the trivial data and toward the information that counts. The example in Figure 7 maps out the

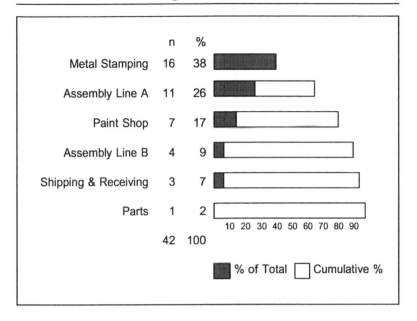

Fig. 7. A Pareto chart.

frequency of time-lost accidents across six different areas within a large production site. The bars across the X or horizontal axis show the number of accidents within each of the individual areas – with the areas being lined up in order starting with the metal stamping area, where we had the most accidents.

What is more interesting, however, is the plotting of the *cumulative* number of accidents across the top of the chart. It answers a very important question – *Which specific areas of the plant are accounting for 80% of our accidents?* Clearly, the answer is the metal stamping area, assembly Line A, and, for some reason, the paint shop. These three areas alone account for 80% of our accidents.

Knowing that, we can direct our ongoing information-gathering activities in a much more focused manner. In effect, it allows us to use a three-stage strategy for gathering information about the problem.

Statistical analysis

Figure 8 shows the correlations between the various dimensions of a personality profile and success in a managerial role. The profile was used to give us a rough picture of the 'personality' which managers were bringing with them into the managerial role, and 'success' was measured using overall performance ratings supplied by the managers' respective superiors.

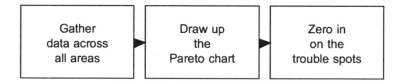

If our 'problem' is to help our middle management team make the transition from a traditional way of managing to a newer, more facilitative style of management – and if *one* part of our strategy for doing so is to make sure that the right people get promoted rather than going by seniority alone – then the data in Figure 8 is clearly going to be relevant. It gives us hard data that we can use to guide our selection and development efforts.

This is **statistical** information. The common thread is that raw information is treated using some sort of statistical transformation, and that the latter presumably allows certain trends or conclusions to stand out clearly in a way that would otherwise be impossible.

	Dimension	*r*
1	Cognitive complexity	.47
2	Action orientation	.42
3	Willingness to bend	-.39
4	Innovativeness	.36
5	Tough-mindedness	.34

Fig. 8. Correlations between personality dimensions
and managerial performance.

Behavioural observation

Actually *watching* people perform their jobs is becoming an increasingly important means of gathering data about both **Fix-It** and **Do-It** problems.

There is no substitute for first-hand observation of a good performer at work. It is the single best way to gain insight into the reality of a job, and into a myriad of specific things that a top performer does that set him or her apart from the average performer. While some of the interviewing is done on a catch-as-catch-can basis during the observational period, it will be important that a proper wrap-up session over coffee be scheduled as well.

The key in the interview is to dig for behavioural specifics and link these to the outcomes produced. If Jim tells us that he *listens well*, we have to come right back and ask him what he means by that. *And how does that make you successful? What does it actually allow you to do or achieve?*

We might find, for example, that Jim listens *actively*. He nods his head from time to time in a way that shows that he is not only listening but *reacting* and *appreciating*. And, periodically, he probes for a bit more detail. He asks the customer to clarify or to expand upon a point. He puts what he has understood into words so that the customer can hear it, confirm it, and then move beyond it.

And how does all this produce outcomes? It builds rapport and rapport builds relationships.

A blank pad of paper

In many ways, the best tool for laying out information is a blank pad of A4 or A3 paper along with a supply of pens and coloured markers.

Lined paper is basically for notes. Unlined paper is basically for pictures. Both are important.

There's a certain art to note-taking. And a great deal to be gained if you get it right. Research at the University of Exeter has shown that taking notes – rather than just reading through some text *without* taking notes – improves one's recall of the material by a factor of six.

Note-taking, done properly, also forces you to *think*. It actively *involves* your intellect in what is going on. It forces you to *work* on it.

Unlined paper is for drawing pictures. And pictures, too, are enormously beneficial. A page filled with boxes and arrows and diamonds and wiggly lines – with just a few words of uppercase text here and there – can often capture the essence of an idea or concept in a way that words all by themselves just can't match.

- A pictorial representation allows us to show and see the interconnections between things. A simple arrow is all that it takes.

- Pictures are better than words at presenting ideas **holistically**. Words are very much a *linear* or *left-brain* form of expression.

- It allows a lot more information to be summarised on a single sheet of paper. A good 80% of text is 'padding' that does not convey meaning.

- We don't have to flip back and forth between page 17 and page 24 as we struggle to relate one part of an overall concept to another.

DO-IT PROBLEMS

Much of what we have been discussing in this chapter applies clearly to our handling of **Fix-It** problems but less obviously to **Do-It** problems. The latter, as we have discussed, involve the *achievement* of something.

It's a problem, in that (1) there is a gap between where we are now and where we want to be and (2) the strategy and means for closing that gap are indeterminate. But it's a more achievement-oriented problem, lending itself to a more proactive approach.

And the focus of our data-gathering in Step Two will be as much on what we want to *achieve* as on the way things are at present. Our concern isn't to pinpoint the *cause* of a problem so much as it is to clarify where we want to get to – what the *solution* will look like, in other words.

What sort of newsletter should it be, for example? What will be its primary purpose? Will distribution be to an internal audience only or will we be sending it out to suppliers and customers as well? What sort of resources do we have to work with? How much can we spend, for example? Enough to bring in an outside consultant? Do we have anyone on board who has done this kind of thing before? Could we perhaps spend a week collecting samples of good newsletters – we seem to get piles of them in the mail every day! – so that we have something to build on? Can we borrow that young lad who works over in marketing – the one who's got the Mac that he brought in from home?

Staying with the newsletter example, an appropriate strategy for our total information-gathering stage might include the following:

- doing some random interviewing to see what employees would like to see in a newsletter

- confirming and expanding upon the above findings using a questionnaire survey to all employees

- talking to the senior people – the directors, and Bob in particular – about their own expectations

- drawing up a few sample pages, each taking a somewhat different angle, and get some reactions

- asking Heather to write away for samples of newsletters from our Training and Development catalogue

- asking Jennifer to collect some technical-type newsletters from next week's trade show in Geneva.

KEY POINTS

- We'll never have time to gather all the information we need about a problem. We have to be selective.

- It's not enough to just gather facts. What's more important is deciding what the facts mean.

- Information-gathering – Step Two of our model – is largely a matter of asking the right questions.

- What, who, why, where, when...these are good words to be using. They're inquisitive words.

- Getting out and *talking* to people is usually the best way to start gathering information.

- It's helpful to talk to a few trusted colleagues individually before getting the whole team together.

- After that – there are many sources of information to tap. Too many, in fact.

- How we represent the facts is crucial. The key is to be able to see things at a glance.

- A force-field analysis is an especially useful way of capturing the dynamics of a problem situation.

- A SWOT model, like all good models, forces us to be comprehensive in our fact-finding.

4
Defining the Problem

Okay, now we have the facts. What – exactly – is the problem? What is not the way it should be?

Defining a problem is tantamount to *understanding* it. Knowing why it's there and what its dynamics are and how it is likely to change between now and next week if we leave it alone.

That's the sort of understanding we'll want to reach by the end of this chapter. And, once we've developed *that* level of clarity about what the problem *is*, we'll probably know what has to be done about it. But unless we get the problem definition step right, any attempt to solve the problem is likely to be futile.

So – what is the problem? What is the *real* problem? That is the question we have to answer.

IDENTIFYING THE GAP

A 'problem', we have said, is a gap between the ways things are and the way they ought to be and 'problem-solving' is how we *close* that gap. It follows, therefore, that our goal at this stage is to understand the two sides of the gap. Only once we have properly defined the gap do we go on to the next stage in the problem-solving cycle and think about how to bridge it.

It might be useful to reproduce our diagram of the problem-solving process which we introduced in Chapter One. We'll insert it here as Figure 9, and we'll do this again from time to time as a way of keeping the model actively in our mind as we work through the various stages.

Figure 10 takes a close-up look at what goes on during Step Three of the problem-solving cycle. All the information that we gathered during Step Two is channelled into one of two boxes.

- The box on the left represents the current state of affairs. We can think of the left as being the 'problem' side of the gap.

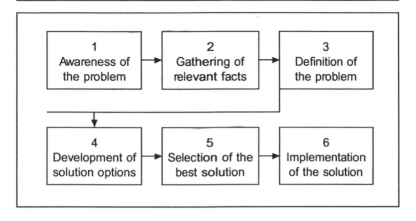

Fig. 9. Problem analysis and solution development.

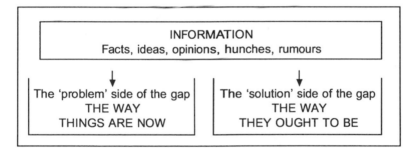

Fig. 10. Information – problem and solution.

• The box on the left represents the current state of affairs. We can think of the left as being the 'problem' side of the gap.

• The box on the right is for information about the way things will be once we solve the problem. We can think of this as being the 'solution' side.

Case study
To illustrate how this works, let's take the problem of developing a system for clipping newspapers. That's a very real problem that Jill Pritchard, one of our *Famous Five* has brought with her from her office-at-home in Chipping Norton. *What is the current situation?* Here's how Jill described things.

'The current situation is that I have newspaper sections and torn-out pages on the coffee table, in the sideboard drawer, in the bathroom. I'll see something that I think I might be able to use in my column, and I'll just tear the whole page out and put it to one side. But I end up with paper all over the place. And when I sit down to write my column, I know there is good material there, lying around somewhere, but I don't have access to it. Trying to find a specific article is too frustrating. There is a feeling of frustration stemming from the fact that all this potential information and all these potential ideas are going to waste.'

Next, we have to define the way things will be done once we've solved the problem. As soon as we have described the way things are right now, we swing right into a description of the way we would like things to be. The reason we do one right after the other is that the two are so closely linked.

Let's return to Jill to tell us how things will be once she's solved her problem.

'How will I know that the problem is solved? I will feel in control of things. Newspaper material will be filed away in some sort of orderly fashion so that I can find or review or scan things when I need to – either searching for a specific article that I can remember or scanning a topic to see what we have on file. The material will be filed away rather than being in view and in the way. The system will be simple to use and I will use it in such a way that newspapers are processed quickly rather than left lying around the house the way they are now.'

Notice that Jill is saying that her clippings will be 'filed away', but she hasn't specified where or how. That will come when we move into the *Solution* phases of the cycle. For now our priority is simply to define the two sides of the gap.

How will I know that the problem is solved?

That's a useful question to ask when searching for a description of the 'solution' side of the gap. Our model – let's keep reminding ourselves – is something that we're actually going to *use*. It has to be natural. The words have to be right. The whole thing has to ring true.

THE FOUR BOXES – SCOC

Let's go a step further – and sub-divide each of the two boxes in Figure 10 into two as shown in Figure 11.

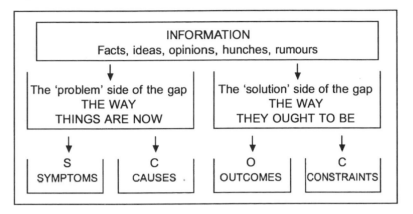

Fig. 11. Information – SCOC.

On the left, we have two boxes for information about the way things are now – the **Symptoms** box and the **Causes** box. On the right, we have the two boxes for information about the way things will be once the problem has been solved – the **Outcomes** box and the **Constraints** box.

When we think about the 'problem' side of the gap our focus will be on separating the symptoms from the causes. As we shift our attention to the other side of the gap – the 'solution' side – our focus will be on fleshing out the outcomes we want to achieve and the constraints which we have to satisfy in doing so.

SYMPTOMS AND CAUSES

The cause of a problem is something that we normally have to *dig* for and the use of the unearthing-the-root analogy is a useful reminder that Step Three of the problem-solving cycle is not an easy one. *Defining* the problem is something else entirely.

CASE STUDY

Lagging sales

To illustrate the importance of asking questions, let's take a classic

Fix-It problem. Sales are down and it's our job to do something about it.

Where does the problem occur, and where does it *not* occur? Here, we have to look at sales figures right across the region – and break them down, if we can, into smaller chunks. If the region is big, then we can ask ourselves whether the falling off in sales has happened more in one part of the region than in others. A big decline in the northwest sector, for example, might be dragging down the figures for the region as a whole.

Maybe our sales are down in those areas where our competitor's sales are up – and the key to the pattern lies in our *competitor's* sales strategies and figures rather than our own. Maybe there's no pattern at all.

How about the *when* question? When does the problem occur and when does it not occur? Is there some sort of pattern here? Are sales figures down during the first half of the month, climbing in the last week but not enough to offset the lacklustre showing of the first three weeks?

Who is involved, and who *isn't* involved? Has there been a uniform dip in sales performance right across the team? Have we *always* had a handful of poor performers? Are the poor results being caused by certain *types* of people?

What precisely is the problem. What is *not* the problem? Sales are down, yes, but can we be more precise about it? What exactly is down? Sales volume? Profit contribution? Sales within certain key produce areas? If it's sales *volume* that is down then let's be clear about that as well. Has there been an absolute decline in sales, or are we talking about sales falling off just a bit against sales *targets* which have risen quite substantially and, perhaps unrealistically? Maybe we're dealing with a product line that is showing its age, and the fault lies with Marketing for not coming up with something to revitalise it.

You can see how tricky it gets. In this specific situation, as it turns out, the *real* problem was eventually defined in the following manner:

'Sales are down because our customers – schools, hospitals, and other institutions – are changing their buying habits. Their decisions are being driven increasingly by economic factors, and the decision-making process itself has become increasingly centralised. We need to take a long, hard look at how the industry is changing and at the implications therefore for our own approach to doing business.'

So that's the problem. The fact that sales are down was just a symptom. The real issue goes a lot deeper and has to do with some rather fundamental questions of change, adaptation and strategy.

IDENTIFYING THE ROOT CAUSE

There is no single best way of getting down to the root cause of a problem. But there *are* some reasonably specific techniques that we may wish to keep in mind.

Asking why

One way to work toward the root cause of a problem is to keep asking ourselves a simple question – **Why?** – until we run out of answers.

Bill: I'm having a problem with Jennifer.
Grace: A 'problem' in what sense?
Bill: I just can't seem to work with her.
Grace: Why is that?
Bill: She seems to have a chip on her shoulder.
Grace: Any idea why that is?
Bill: I think – I'm not sure, but I think – she wanted the job over in Marketing that Joanne ended up getting.
Grace: Why is that? Why did she want the job so badly?
Bill: The challenge, I suppose. It's something different. It's a good career move.
Grace: And why should not getting the job cause her to go around with a chip on her shoulder?
Bill: I think she felt she deserved it more than Joanne.
Grace: Why?
Bill: Uh, I'm not sure. I think she just felt that she was better qualified to do the job.

Grace is backing Bill up, level by level, until he runs out of answers. If she's really astute, she might come back with something like this.

For what's it worth, Bill, I think Joanne was the right person for that job. The whole role of marketing has changed so much in the past year, and I don't know that Jennifer has the sort of strategic skills that we were looking for. More to the point, I'm not sure that Jennifer knows that. I think she needs to be helped to understand exactly what was needed in the marketing role, and why – and, as managers, we generally don't do a very good job of educating people along those lines.'

Asking the 'not' question

When scientists want to isolate and identify the cause of a problem, they often compare an experimental group of subjects with a control group of subjects. Everything about the two groups is identical except for a single condition or characteristic – the one being explored.

We can set up the same sort of comparison in the way we ask our *where*, *when*, *who*, and *what* questions:

- Where does the problem occur?

- Where does it *not* occur?

- When does the problem occur?

- When does it *not* occur?

- Who is involved in the problem situation?

- Who is *not* involved?

- What precisely is the problem?

- What is *not* the problem?

If the problem is that people on one team are unhappy why aren't people on the *other* teams unhappy? Perhaps they are, but haven't said so. Maybe there's only *one* person on the team who is unhappy but who is affecting the others.

But – maybe there's something about being on that team that is the root cause of the problem. We don't jump to any conclusions, but neither do we ignore what the evidence is suggesting to us.

CASE STUDY

Morale on Ward Four

Morale amongst the nurses on Ward Four is poor. That's the problem.

So how do we *define* the problem? A group of personnel officers were asked that very question. One of them commented –

'The problem is poor morale amongst the nurses.'

True, but does that *define* the problem? Or, by using the term 'poor morale', are we simply putting a label on the symptoms? Another participant offered the following:

'The real cause is probably a combination of things – low pay, the fact of being held to a 2.5 per cent increase, a lack of influence over how certain things on the ward are done, and then just the constant pressure of dealing with people who are ill...'

That's a more analytical way of looking at things, and it is very tempting to stop right there and ask 'Okay, now what are some of the possible solutions we can look at?' – in other words, to accept that we've defined the problem (Step Three) and are ready to start looking for solutions (Step Four).

But there's one obvious problem.

The nurses on Wards Two and Three are also working under the same conditions and don't seem to have a 'morale' problem. It's only on Ward Four.

Why Ward Four?

It's such an easy trap to fall into. And it underscores the advantage of asking ourselves not just *where* a problem is occurring but where is it *not* occurring...not just *when* the problem shows itself but when does it *not* show itself. Why is there *not* a morale problem on Wards Two and Three?

SOME MORE TECHNIQUES

Asking a series of 'why' questions. Asking the 'not' question. We've introduced these as specific 'techniques'. Let's add on a few more.

Testing our hypotheses
It will be helpful to think of our ideas about the root *cause* of a problem as being **hypotheses**. Doing so implies that they have to be tested out in some way. *If X is the cause, then Y should hold true.*

If the rather marked decline in our export business is being caused by the sustained strength of the pound, then historical data should show that our export business has been strongest when the pound has been weakest.

Arguing with ourselves

This technique involves introducing a rule – every time we come up with something that we think is the real cause of the problem, another part of us has to play devil's advocate and try to refute it. In our case study, if low wages were the cause, the morale problem would be found on Ward Two and Ward Three as well, not just Ward Four – so, no, low wages can't be the cause of the problem.

Taking action – hypothetically

The idea here is to play out a solution in our mind and see whether it solves the problem.

If I fix this, will it solve the problem? If the answer is either –

● no, it won't

● no, not necessarily

– then we should continue our search for the real cause.

If the fall-off in business out of the Dublin office is the result of Brenda's leadership then replacing her with a stronger manager should produce an increase in business. *Would it?* If we can imagine someone else taking over from Brenda, do our instincts tell us that the results would demonstrate a significant improvement?

Why? What would someone else do that would cause the situation to change?

The point is this. We can't afford to move ahead on the basis of blind faith. There's too much at stake. So we have to tread carefully. Unless we can make a convincing case for the idea that replacing Brenda will solve the problem, then we need to keep working on our definition of the problem.

Drawing a picture

We have talked before about the usefulness of representing information pictorially.

The very act of *drawing* the picture is often enough to bring the causal relationships in a complex situation out into the open where we can see them. Slowly but surely, as we do this, we begin to get a sense of how things hang together. We begin to see what causes what, and where the change levers are. We begin to *understand* the situation.

OUTCOMES AND CONSTRAINTS

There are two classes of criteria that a solution will have to satisfy – **outcomes** and **constraints**. Outcomes are results which our chosen solution will have to produce. Constraints are limits within which we have to operate. We need to be as clear and specific as we can about the end result we are after.

OUTCOMES

The **outcome** is the total end result we are trying to achieve.

The process of identifying and articulating the real outcome in a *Do-It* situation is very much like the process of identifying the root cause of a *Fix-It* problem. It involves asking the *Why* question again and again until we arrive at something that has the ring of finality about it.

Case study

The real objective
It is important that we define the *real* objective we are trying to achieve. Tony Martindale, one of our *Famous Five* and the director of sales and marketing for one of the country's most dynamic packaged foods companies makes his contribution:

'One of my people – Susan – had taken it upon herself to create a resource library. It was added to her annual objectives as a one-off goal. At the end of the year, when we were doing her performance appraisal, I raised the issue of the library. Susan was surprised because the library thing was done – an empty office had been converted to a resource room stocked with a good supply of books and magazines and resource material. But I pointed out to Susan that no one was using it. I hadn't seen one person actually go into the library, and it's just down the hall from my office. Was that our objective, I asked Susan – to create a really impressive library that no one uses? Or was the real objective to get our people reading more, or to inject some new ideas into our thinking, or to get people to look at what other companies are doing before they commit us to a course of action? What was the actual outcome that we wanted to achieve, and why was it important? Susan hadn't really stopped to ask herself that question.'

A good question to be asking ourselves is *What is the actual outcome that we want to achieve, and why is it important?* And the answer might be – *So our people will have ready access to relevant books and journals and internal reports and market data.* But then the follow-up question. Why is that important? *Because we want our people to be making decisions on the basis of the best possible data and intelligence.* And why is that? *Because the problems they are dealing with are getting more and more complex and the need for up-to-date intelligence is more acute.*

And recognising this is useful. The person who is out to develop a resource library is going to do things one way. The person who is out to better equip our people to deal with an increasingly complex environment will do things in another. Their respective mindsets will have a very real bearing on the way they approach the project.

CONSTRAINTS

Develop a resource library and –

• have it done by the end of the month

• don't spend more than £1,000

• don't knock any walls down.

There are some simple constraints as distinct from 'outcomes'. **Constraints** are usually limits in terms of five main resources:

• time
• space
• money
• materials
• people.

Constraints also may involve limits on the range of acceptable solutions.

• The solution has to be acceptable to the directors because it needs their approval.

• The projected increase in profit contribution should be at least 15 per cent.

• The design of the product has to be consistent with standards being introduced by our US parent.

KEY POINTS

- Defining a problem is tantamount to understanding it. Knowing why it is there and how it is likely to change if we leave it alone.

- And, once we've developed that level of clarity about what the problem *is*, we will probably know what has to be done about it.

- Unless we get the problem definition step right, any attempt to solve the problem is likely – ultimately if not immediately – to be futile.

- Our goal at this stage is to articulate and understand the two sides of the gap – the way things are now and the way they will be once we've solved the problem.

- On the way-things-are-now side of the gap, we need to gather information about, and identify, the symptoms and the causes of the problem.

- On the way-things-ought-to-be side of the gap, we need to think about, and identify, the outcomes to be achieved and the constraints to be met.

- There is no single best way of getting down to the root cause of a problem. There is no single technique that will work in every situation.

- One way to work toward the root cause of a problem is to keep asking ourselves a simple question – why? – until we run out of answers.

- It will be helpful to think of our ideas about the root cause of a problem as being hypotheses which need to be tested out in some way.

- The most common way to test an hypothesis is through the simple application of logic. If X is the cause, then Y should hold true.

- Outcomes are results which our chosen solution will have to produce. Constraints are limits within which we have to operate.

- If our problem is a *Fix-It* problem, we'll spend most of our Step 2 and Step 3 time on the symptoms and causes side of the gap.

- If our problem is a *Do-It* problem, we'll spend most of our Step 2 and Step 3 time on the outcomes and constraints side of the gap.

- But the challenge is the same in both cases. We need to understand where we are starting from, and where we want to get to.

5
Developing Solution Options

At this point, then, we've defined the problem. Now...we're ready to move on to that portion of the problem-solving cycle where the *solution*, not the problem, takes the spotlight.

The solution will usually not be obvious. So we have more hard work ahead of us – and the quality of the solution we ultimately select will only be as high as the quality of the solution options we generate and examine.

SOME GUIDELINES TO KEEP IN MIND

What we want to do is simply make sure, before we go on, that every solution worth looking at has been put on the table.

Let's consider five guidelines that will help us do that.

1. Focus on feasibility

The solution of a problem rarely calls upon us to consider every single option. If the problem is something as mundane as choosing a vacation, it seems obvious that we don't give active consideration to every single vacation spot in the *world* before making our final choice.

So we're looking for options which are *feasible* and which promise to deliver the outcomes we have targeted and satisfy the constraints within which we are operating.

2. Boil it down to two alternatives

Once we have done a first cut and moved from all those options which are *possible* to considering only those which are *feasible*, we'll still have our hands full.

Ideally, we would like to narrow it down to a choice between two options, both of which are attractive and will get the job done. It might be three. It could be four. But once we get to five it becomes difficult. Two makes for a nice, natural decision. Three is probably the practical limit.

3. Don't neglect the do-nothing option

Deciding not to decide is always an option. You can leave the problem unsolved either because you think it's not worth solving, that it will solve itself, or now is not the best time to do it. So, in thinking about solution options, we have to ask the question – Do we need to take action at all? Is there a chance that we'll make things *worse* by meddling?

Never choose the do-nothing option simply because you can't think of anything better to do. Choose it for a specific reason which you can articulate.

Examining ways of doing nothing

What we're calling the **do-nothing** option doesn't always mean doing *nothing* nor is it necessarily an option to be avoided.

- *Monitor the situation.* If the problem is not an urgent one then a decision to simply monitor the situation is certainly justifiable.

- *Treat the symptoms.* Do this when the symptoms demand an urgent response even though a tackling of the underlying cause cannot be done quickly.

- *Make a temporary decision.* Do something quickly, but make it a move designed to buy time.

- *Make a conditional decision.* Make the decision but stop short of moving on to the implementation stage until the decision is needed.

4. Trying to think 'outside the box'

Let's just talk briefly about what creativity is – and its role in the whole problem-solving process.

For the benefit of this illustration we'll take the example of creative thinking – the joining-the-dots problem from which stems the description of creative thinking as **thinking outside the box**. The problem is simple. You have to join all the dots in a 3 × 3 matrix using only three lines. The solution involves quite literally *thinking outside the box*.

Let's think about what thinking outside the box means. It means that the solution is somehow outside the range of solutions we would have initially considered.

And *why* is it outside? Because it breaks a rule we've been following in our thinking. In the case of the nine-dots problem, the rule is that our straight lines can't extend beyond the box formed by the nine dots.

The key point is this – creativity isn't just a matter of brainstorming. It also means releasing our mind from the shackles and boundaries which keep it from wandering to far afield. This means asking questions which seem a bit too 'obvious' to be worth asking. For example:

- Is this problem worth solving?
- Is it really a 'problem'?
- What if we just told them the truth?
- What if we just forgot about the whole thing and went back to work?
- What if we just went ahead and launched the product anyway?

5. Looking for the logic in the situation
In most problem-solving situations **clear** thinking is more important than **creative** thinking.

Figure 12 shows that addressing the main issue is a good example of thinking **logically** about a problem, and allowing the logic inherent in the problem itself to suggest the appropriate solution.

If the main issue is	then it makes sense to think in terms of
that our support people don't take the spending guidelines *seriously* enough...	doing something tangible to drive home the point that we really mean business
the lack of communication between the Engineering and Logistics people...	breaking down the barrier between these groups before we do anything else
the *packaging* of the idea, rather than its content per se or the logic behind it...	bringing in a marketing expert rather than spending more money on the design consultants

Fig. 12. Thinking logically about a problem.

SOME GOOD QUESTIONS TO ASK

Now let's look at some useful **questions** which will help ensure that every solution worth looking at has been put on the table.

1. What did we do the last time?

If the problem has occurred before let's not jump to the conclusion that we should do exactly the same thing again but let's put that solution on our list of options to be considered.

We must also keep the following points in mind:

- The two situations may *look* the same but contain some very subtle differences.

- What worked last time may not work as well this time.

- There's always a chance that we chose the *wrong* solution last time – but it just happened to work.

- There's a good chance that what we did last time was an adequate solution but not an optimal one.

2. What did our competitors do?

We're being hit hard by smaller and more nimble competitors. That's the problem we have to explore, analyse, define, and solve.

If our major competitors have faced the same problem, then it makes sense to find out as much as we can about what they did to solve it and why.

But we'll need to be geared up for this type of intelligence-gathering. If none of us has a good contact in the competitor's camp, then we've got to find a way to develop one.

3. Will this actually solve the problem?

Options have to be *explored* – not just identified. It is worth taking a few minutes to think each one through.

What this does is bring the option to life. And that, in turn, helps us more properly evaluate just what the option will do for us in practice.

THE MOST COMMON PITFALLS

Let's go through some of the most common pitfalls when our attention turns to the development of solution options. Three stand out.

1. Not considering all the options

The most common mistake that we tend to make is not taking time to explore and develop all the options which are available to us.

We seem to forget that information-gathering and thinking are just as legitimate as the more glamorous and attention-getting act of making a decision.

2. Searching for the 'right' solution

In most situations, it is going to be very difficult to decide on a solution if we worry too much about finding the *right* solution.

What we need to look for are solutions that will work. They don't have to be perfect. They just have to be realistic, workable, manageable solutions.

3. Sticking with the tried and true

Settling for the safe range of options when something a lot more exciting is what the situation requires is the problem here.

This implies that we're ignoring a blatant call for creativity by putting on our blinkers. We're not. It's just that we're operating under pressure.

THINKING STRATEGICALLY

Too often, we move from goal-setting to action-taking without stopping to develop a general **strategy**.

Case study

Mary Slater, account manager with one of the country's leading office supplies manufacturers, talks here about her effort to win the chain's total own-brand business away from the competition.

'It's taken the better part of a year-and-a-half, getting them to the point where we're now talking about us supplying their own-brand school supplies and household stationery items. For the first two months I kept hammering away at this person and then that person, telling them how great our products were and how we could bring their costs down and all the usual things that I am sure they hear from every potential supplier.

It was only after two months of flailing around that Frank, my regional manager, told me to take a few days off and develop a proper business plan. He used the idea of 'thinking back-wards'...starting out by visualising the end result I wanted to achieve and then working backward to see how I got there. And he emphasised the fact that the strategy had to be right. The overall approach. That was the secret.'

Thinking strategically. Let's see if we can find out what Mary's boss was getting at.

A lot of us, when faced with a problem are inclined to skip over a very important step. We leap from the **goal** to the **action plan**. What we're skipping over is the development of a **strategy**.

Here's Mary again:

'To land a new account, or get an existing customer to take on a new product, there are several different strategies I can use. I can go in there aggressively and trust that my own confidence and enthusiasm and leadership – backed by my company's track record for quality products – will be enough to produce a positive decision on their part. Or, I can put together a comprehensive financial analysis that lays out current and projected costs and benefits. One of our accounting people can handle the gathering of data and we probably have some presentation software that will allow us to put our case forward in a convincing fashion.'

That's what we mean by 'strategy'. It cuts down on the amount of work we have to do and increases the likelihood of our getting things right.

Cutting down on the amount of work

We're going on holiday.

Having resolved that, I am left with a problem of deciding where to go. It will mean laying out an array of options, weighing their respective pros and cons, choosing one, and then making the final arrangements.

I have a box of travel brochures at home, there's a tourist office nearby, I've been saving newspaper clippings about places to visit. I'll also get the travel section from the newspapers...

That's me. Moving into action. But I'm going to stop myself this time. I'm going to think *strategically. What* sort *of vacation do we want?*

We want a relaxing family vacation and we'll talk about it over supper tonight. We can think about it and make a final decision by the weekend.

So – I'm *not* going to turn the house upside down with piles of newspaper clippings for the Greek Islands, for Mauritius and for Scotland.

No, it has to be a relaxing family vacation. Clarifying that cuts out hours of work and addresses the whole question of strategy. Not *Where do we go for our vacation?* But *What's the best way to decide?*

Helping to get things right

Thinking strategically also helps us get things right.

Do we want to talk 'partnership' with them or threaten to take them to court?

This is a *strategic* question. It invites you to choose a class or category of solution before looking at specific options. It will cut down on the amount of time we'll have to spend analysing our options.

DEVELOPING A SINGLE OPTION

You might be a bit worried at this stage. *What's all this about developing a range of options?*

Don't fret. Jennifer Adair, one of our *Famous Five*, had this to say:

> 'In most situations, I don't think the idea of lining up a whole range of options is realistic. At least it doesn't describe the way things happen in my own experience. Most of my time is spent developing and testing out and refining a single solution. Why try to think of five ways to solve a problem when it only takes one good solution? So I'm asking myself all the time – How am I going to solve this thing? What's the best thing to do?

Managers don't always generate a **range** of solutions. They struggle with the problem and, slowly but surely, they start to settle on and build a solution. It takes shape slowly, with a lot of re-working along the way. But it's all one solution – continually evolving and changing shape, yes, but still one single solution.

So let's keep that in mind as we go onto the next step in our problem-solving cycle: choosing the best solution.

KEY POINTS

• Our goal in Step 4 is not to choose a solution. It is simply to make sure that every solution worth looking at has been put on the table.

- The solution will usually not be obvious. If it were, someone would surely have implemented it by now and solved the problem.

- We are looking for options which are feasible – which are do-able within the limits of the situation and using the resources at our disposal.

- Ideally, we would like to narrow it down to a choice between two options, both of which are attractive and will get the job done.

- Deciding not to decide is always an option. In thinking about solution options, we have to ask the question – Do we need to take action at all?

- Never choose the do-nothing option just because you can't think of anything better to do. Choose it for a specific reason which you can articulate.

- Creativity means 'thinking outside the box' – thinking along lines which go against established assumptions and break with traditional mindsets.

- Thinking strategically – defining a general space within which to define or search for options – is an important part of the problem-solving process.

- Not considering all the options, and confining our options to a narrow and conservative range, are two of the most common pitfalls at this stage.

- In practice, we won't always generate a range of options. We may spend our time building and fine-tuning what it is effect a single option.

6
Choosing the Best Solution

We're at a stage now where a decision has to be made and it is here that judgement, business sense and intuition come into play.

AN EFFECTIVE DECISION

An **effective** decision, or an effective solution, is one which accomplishes the intended result.

There are several strategies. All will apply to most problem-solving situations. All can and should be used concurrently.

- Get the process right.
- Test out the decision – mentally.
- Test out the decision – in practice.
- Put it in words.
- Get the right people involved.
- Assess and cover the risks.
- Get the timing right.
- Don't let decisions become rules.

Getting the process right

Bad decisions occur because of a weakness in the problem-solving cycle. There are *so* many places where just a slight miscalculation can result in our choosing a solution which turns out to be sub-optimal.

> *Let's make sure we get the process right.*
> **That is a mantra that we should be repeating to ourselves over and over again until we get sick of hearing it.**

Testing out the decision – mentally
Sketching out an action plan focuses our mind on the practical details. It's a good way, too, to look at the risks that might be involved.

In effect, it's a good way to **test out** our solution – give it a trial run before committing ourselves to it.

And – what happens if something goes wrong? Can we still get the thing done by the deadline date?

Testing out the decision – in practice
Some decisions lend themselves to an actual testing process.

• Putting a new control system in place in one part of the factory to assess how well it works.

• Having a sampling of users in three departments try out a new software programme for one week.

• Putting a merchandising display unit in a handful of stores to see how customers react.

At other times, 'testing' a decision involves trying it out on one or two key people before taking it to the group as a whole.

This is important in situations where the decision needs to be vetted or approved by other people – the board of directors, for example.

And that, in turn, allows us to go in better equipped and more confident of coming away with what we want.

Putting it in words
Never make a decision without talking it through with at least one person or writing it down for someone else to read. In other words – never make a decision in isolation.

Getting the right people involved
Their knowledge, experience and expertise may be needed to provide sound, authoritative advice or at least know how to go about finding an answer to a problem.

There is also the whole issue of ownership and commitment. We'll want people to actually feel a sense of commitment to a project and to have some sort of stake in its successful implementation. They have to be involved ... the earlier in the problem-solving process the better.

Really think this one through carefully. Whose commitment will be essential? Whose input will be needed? And when, exactly, should these people be brought into the loop?

Assessing and covering the risks

There is an element of *risk* in most decision-making situations, and we need to be as clear as we can about what the risks are and how they can be minimised.

- What can go wrong?

- What are the chances of that happening?

- How serious would the consequences be?

- What steps would we take to deal with them?

- Can we reduce the likelihood of it happening?

- What is the *worst* possible thing that could happen?

- Are we prepared to live with that?

What's the worst thing that can happen? That's an especially useful question, and it's always best to answer it in some detail. And then – *Are we prepared to live with it? Can you or your client absorb the worst-case-scenario loss?* That's the issue.

Getting the timing right

The world seems to move more quickly every day and we have to respond accordingly. It's not so much that decisions themselves need to be made more quickly; it's that the problem-solving process – of which the *act* of decision-making is but one part – has to be more attuned to what is happening.

- We can't afford to get bogged down in data analysis. If the computer can do it, let the computer do it.

- Intelligence – knowing what is going on – is crucial. The manager has to know what is happening.

- We have to keep a close eye on what is happening *outside* our organisation, in the industry at large.

- There is no room for procrastination. The cost of delay is getting higher and higher all the time.

Sometimes, yes, our decisions will have to be made more quickly because they have to keep pace with the increased cost of delay. There are times when we have to not only make the right decision but be *quick* about it as well.

But the key point is that the problem-solving cycle as a whole has to be more responsive to the sheer speed with which things happen and change. Our sensitivity to and awareness of potential problems have to be sharper, crisper, keener, and more effective now than ever before.

Don't let decisions become rules

Decisions have a way of becoming rules if we allow them to. What starts out as a solution to a problem – *How do we get this package to its recipient by noontime tomorrow despite having missed the daily pick-up at the post office?* – becomes a routine solution that we fall back on any time the problem arises. We call the overnight courier people, where we've established an account.

Some solutions deserve to be routinised, and the above is a good example.

> **The trouble begins when we routinise things that shouldn't be routinised – when we allow *routines* to become a substitute for *thinking*.**

DECIDING HOW TO DECIDE

It is often useful to articulate the general **strategy** we will use for making a decision. A hiring decision, for example:

- We're going to hire the first candidate who can do the job. The key thing is to get someone in there quickly.

- I want the best possible person for the job. If I have to talk to fifty people and reject them I'll do that.

- It's attitude I'm after. The technical side of things is something we can teach.

- I won't hire anyone who doesn't have growth potential.

These are four different ways of approaching this and each will put its stamp on how the decision is made and what sort of person is ultimately hired.

The usefulness of articulating the strategy we are using is that we make it conscious. We *decide* to use it rather than allowing it to operate in the background without our awareness.

TAKING THE LOGICAL ROUTE

Graeme Weir, one of our *Famous Five*, was quite candid in assessing himself as a decision-maker:

'I'm not a quick decision-maker, and I don't like being in situations where I feel pressured to make a quick decision. I guess it's the Engineer in me – I like to have time to sift through the facts and look at the various options and weigh the pros and cons and not move ahead until I'm pretty sure of my ground. That's just the way I am, and I've got to say that I've been pretty successful over the years operating that way. But making snap decisions? Putting out fires? No, that's not something that I'm especially good at.

How does Graeme actually make decisions?

'I tend to be quite logical about most things. Again, I think what you're seeing is the effect of my training as an Engineer. If I can quantify something – assign values – I will. I do it because it's a good way to discipline the mind, even in situations like hiring where the factors and criteria are relatively loose and subjective.'

Let's have Graeme talk us through an actual example. There are three young candidates being assessed and Graeme starts by using a grid – we have reproduced it here as Figure 13 and pointing to the right-hand column.

'I look at six main things – the quality and relevance of their education, the extent to which they have practised what I call continuous learning on their own time, their ability to relate to people and work on a team, their brightness in the interview and in solving various problems during the assessment, their knowledge of our business, and their attitude.'

	V	Larkin		Jones		Stevens	
		R	VR	R	VR	R	VR
Education	1	3	3	3	3	2	2
Learning	2	2	4	1	2	1	2
People skills	2	1	2	2	4	1	2
Brightness	2	3	6	2	4	2	4
Knowledge	1	2	2	3	3	2	2
Attitude	3	2	6	3	9	2	6
TOTAL			23		25		18

Fig. 13. Assessment criteria for job interviews.

He continues:

'These, if you like, are the criteria. I've given each one a value – in the V column – according to how important I think it is as a factor affecting the decision. On a scale from 1 to 3, I've rated Attitude a 3 because it's the one thing I can't teach or train someone. They have to bring it in with them. Things like Education and Knowledge get a 1 – which means that they are important but I'm willing to make a deal.'

So there are six **criteria**. And we've assigned a value to each. Then we turn our attention to the candidates:

'I rate each candidate on each criterion. Again, I keep it simple – a rating from 1 to 3, recorded in the R column. Then I multiply the value of V by the value of R. The importance of the criterion times the likelihood that the candidate will satisfy that criterion. Then, when I've done all that, I simply add up the figures in the VR column to get an overall score for each candidate.'

RELYING ON OUR INSTINCTS

The other way to make a decision is to trust our instincts. Jack Carter, another one of our *Famous Five*, was facing a tough hiring decision. The approach that he took could not have been more different.

'I've learned to trust my instincts in a situation like this. No matter how much information you gather about a candidate, no matter how many hours you spend interviewing, no matter how many referees you speak to, it still boils down to a gut feel decision once you narrow things down to the top three or four candidates. I won't hire anyone unless I'm excited about getting them on board and turning them loose.'

We asked Jack if there is a conflict between trusting one's instincts and the much more structured approach that we saw in Graeme Weir.

'Most often, my instincts just confirm what the facts are telling me. But there are times, yes, when I've got to go with the one or the other – and, when that happens, I generally go with what my instincts are telling me. On those occasions when I haven't, I've paid the price every time. When I've trusted my gut feel – my decision to hire Susan is a good example – it almost always worked out well.'

Susan Beal?

'Her background was all wrong. If I had been using an agency or a recruiting firm, Susan would never have come to my attention. She didn't have any industry experience, she was light in terms of management experience, and her exposure to our type of organisational structure was virtually nil. But there was something about her CV that caught my attention. The fact that she had taken a shot a setting up her own business and won a major contract with BAT. The year she spent working as a special assistant to the Chairman when she was with Northbridge. Her involvement in the AT&T deal. I looked at what she had actually *done* – as opposed to the job titles she had had – and I thought to myself "Boy, this is an Achiever!". So I had her come in for an interview. And ten minutes after she walked into my office, I knew my instincts had been right. Now, two months later, I'm more convinced than ever.'

Trusting our instincts means letting our own mental computer chew on the data and then tell us what to do. Yes. There's a little black box inside us somewhere that functions very much like a computer. Our black box takes the facts of the situation and then carries out a computational process which is probably not unlike the decision matrix that Graeme uses. The end result is that we know, instinctively, how something sits with us. A final word from Jack Carter:

'I don't want it to sound as if I'm pulling decisions out of a hat, because I'm not. I do think about things, and I try to be quite systematic about it. But, at the end of the day, when I have to total up my thoughts and make an overall decision, I would rather go for a walk in the park than sit at my desk and add up a bunch of figures. Walking through the park, I get a sense of which direction I'm leaning in – and I've learned to pay attention to that sense and trust it. Sitting at a desk, all I've got is a bunch of figures. And, to me, decision-making at this level isn't about adding up figures; it's about judgement.'

PITFALLS AT THE SOLUTION SELECTION STAGE

Deciding without deciding
The non-decision:

Jane: You should probably let Bill know that we're thinking of re-activating the idea. He may want to sit in on the Tuesday meeting.
Harry: Yeah, I suppose so. I'll think about it.

We probably do this more than we realise. We make decisions by not making decisions. *I'll do it later. I'll get back to you.* These are all ways of **deciding not to decide** but it still has the full force of a decision. It won't stop other people from making *their* decisions. But by that time, the matter will be out of our hands. Our chance to be proactive, to make a difference, will have come and gone.

Regarding a decision as 'final'
Another common pitfall is that of closing off the entire problem-solving cycle on the assumption that a decision has been made.
The problem is that we live in a very fluid world and a decision that looked good last week may present difficulties this week and we

could end up with a worse problem on our hands than we started with.

Some of us still feel that changing our mind is, somehow, a sign of weakness. But not today. We'll just have to keep an eye on things and be prepared to re-activate the whole problem-solving cycle if the need to do so is there. What we can *not* do is paste the label 'final' on this or any other solution we come up with.

Waiting until all the facts are in

The problem is, of course, all the facts are *never* in. Things change so rapidly these days that by the time the last facts come in, the first facts will probably be obsolete.

Plus – there's an assumption being made that having all the facts at our disposal will somehow tell us what to *do* about a problem. The 'facts' will make a decision for us. We'll be off the hook.

Things don't happen that way. And the cost of gathering every last scrap of information about a problem would be prohibitive.

Relying too much on 'gut feel'

There's a time and a place and a proper role for instincts and intuition in the problem-solving process but we don't want to carry it too far.

The manager who boasts, or states with conviction that their gut feeling is providing the direction to an important decision is suspect.

Trusting our instincts isn't something we should boast about or do with conviction. It is something we should do cautiously, prudently, and humbly.

Not looking at the big picture

Tunnel vision is the problem here. Choosing an option that quite adequately satisfies the local or immediate criteria but falls short when weighed against the demands or constraints of the wider and longer-term context.

A classic example is the short-sighted career decision, which we'll call *The Case of the Greener Pastures*.

CASE STUDY

Greener pastures

Careers seem to be a constant source of both satisfaction and problems. One of the most common phenomena is the lure of the greener pastures. Witness Andrew Putnam:

'I wasn't dreadfully unhappy. I've got to say that right at the outset. I had done well in a straight selling role at Mars and I moved quickly into sales management. And as a training ground, it was probably the best company that anyone could ever work for. But June and I were mortgaged up to the hilt and we had a second child on the way and, at the same time and because of the quick strides I had made, I was probably getting a bit of an exaggerated sense of my own worth on the market. I can remember joking with June about the fact that, if footballers could move around from club to club every couple of years and end up earning £50,000 a week and driving a Porsche, then why shouldn't I be doing the same sort of thing.'

The 'problem' came in the form of a rather flattering job offer that was difficult to ignore.

'I had lunch with a headhunter who had somehow gotten my name and seemed to know all about what I had done at Mars. And I must say I felt rather flattered by the whole situation. To make a long story short, I ended up moving to a small company that was importing and distributing breads and biscuits and pastas from Italy. I liked the people who were running the business and the whole thing had an entrepreneurial flavour to it that was really exciting. Plus, it have me a chance to really challenge myself and make my mark. My lofty title was Director of Sales and Marketing, there was a rather nice company car involved – a BMW, and the financial package was, as they say, too good to turn down. So away I went.'

That was three years ago and it was an ill-advised move.

'A year-and-a-half into the job, I knew I had made a mistake. In fact, I knew it within months. Sure, the money and the title were there, but I was effectively working – and working awfully damned hard – as a glorified sales rep, calling on the independents and the regional chains and hustling to get our product in there. Meanwhile, the whole industry was changing in some very dramatic and exciting ways, with the multiples taking a bigger and bigger share of the pie and getting themselves involved in everything from banking to selling computers. And I was missing out.'

Remember that we've defined a 'problem' as a gap between the way things are and the way we would want them to be. Andrew has just described the first half of the gap. Here's the second:

'What I really wanted to do was call on Tesco. Or Sainsbury's. Or Safeways. I wanted to be back in the big leagues, doing business on a large scale, working with the big national accounts. If you're in consumer products, then that's where the excitement is. That's where the growth is. That's where you get involved with the companies and the people who are driving the whole industry. And if you're *good* at what you do, that's where you want to compete.'

KEY POINTS

• The test of a decision is whether or not it delivers the goods. Whether it solves the problem.

• Get the process right. That is a mantra that we should repeat to ourselves over and over again.

• Decisions should be tested out – mentally or in practice – before we commit to them.

• It helps immensely to talk a decision through with someone, or to write it out on paper.

• Get the right people involved – those whose commitment will drive the process.

• Look at everything that can go wrong. Assess the risks and make sure you are prepared to cover them.

• Get the timing right. In today's fast-moving world, that usually means moving more quickly.

• Don't allow one-off decisions to harden into rules and routines unless you do it consciously.

• Use quantitative tools, by all means, but they aren't a substitute for thinking and/or judgement.

• Assess workability. Don't just look at the logic of a solution. It has to work in practice.

• You don't have to weigh every single option. Most managers in most situations don't.

- Don't waste time looking for the right decision. Nine times out of ten, there is no such thing.

- Don't sit and wait until 'all the facts are in'. That is simply never going to happen.

- When a decision has to be made, make it. Don't waffle or temporise or run and hide.

- But don't, on the other hand, declare that a decision is 'Final!'. Very few decisions are final.

7
Implementing the Solution

The decision by itself doesn't solve the problem. We have to translate the decision into an effective plan of action – and execute it.

- What, specifically, is the goal of the proposed action?
- What action steps are involved?
- What's the schedule?
- Who is responsible for monitoring and expediting those steps?
- Who has to be involved at each step along the way?
- What resources will be needed?
- What intelligence will be needed?
- What costs will be involved?
- Who is responsible for managing the total implementation cycle?
- Who is accountable for the project?
- Is everyone on board?

BUILDING A VISUAL PLAN

Unless the actions we propose to take are very simple and few in number, we would be wise to develop a visual overview of our total action plan. This will help us work through the sequence of events and spot potential conflicts on the way.

At times, a simple schedule of events will do. At other times, we'll need a proper flow chart that shows how the various steps will link up and overlap. We need to keep it as simple as possible but complex and flexible enough to do the job.

A **visual plan** (Figure 14) is one approach that seems to work well. It breaks the total solution into a series of major action *chunks* and plots them on a planning calendar so that they can be seen at a glance.

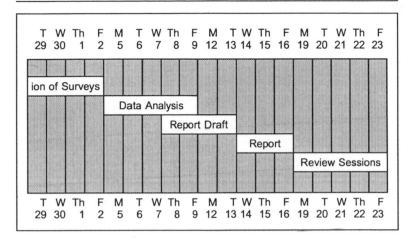

Fig. 14. Visual plan and overview of the action plan.

1. Define the objective

This is about the end result that the project has to accomplish and the date by which that has to be done.

2. Identify the major chunks

Next, we break the project down into its major component parts. Each part should be a **chunk** of activity with an identifiable beginning and end – data analysis, for example, to be done during the week of the 5th – and the parts, when strung together end to end, should add up to the successful completion of the project as a whole.

3. Define a goal for each chunk

It is useful to define a major **goal** for each of these chunks.

That will normally mean that something is finalised, produced and, in most cases, delivered.

4. Attach a target date to each

Once our goals have been defined, we attach a target date to each such that the project will come to a successful completion on time.

5. Develop an action plan for each goal

On a separate form like the one shown in Figure 15, each goal can then be broken down into its component action steps, with each step being assigned its own specific target date. They are what will guide our day-to-day, hour-by-hour activities.

	Action	Deadline
Label:		
Goal:		
1		
2		
3		
4		
5		
6		
7		
8		

Fig. 15. Action plan.

THE ART OF DELEGATION

The rationale for delegating is very straightforward. A successful manager rests heavily on the principle of **leverage**. Exercising leverage means multiplying your impact. Making a decision that affects how ten different people will go about their jobs is a high-leverage activity. There are two classes of activity in which you – as a manager – should be engaged:

- things which have a widespread impact extending beyond your own personal work

- things which require your unique managerial perspective and status.

There is a second factor with delegation – decisions about what to do are best taken by those closest to the scene of the action. The closer we get to the scene of the action, the more specific and up-to-date is the information on which the problem-solving will be based. And then, of course, there is a third factor which often involves more work than a single person can handle. It requires a co-ordinated team effort.

1. Delegating by results
This is perhaps the most important principle of effective delegation – don't give people tasks to do, give them a result to achieve.

- Make sure that the objective, and the date by which it has to be achieved, are absolutely clear.

- Spell out when you should be consulted or when initiative is to be exercised (see Figure 16).

- Give the other person your 'feel' for the problem in hand.

- Ask the individual to prepare a plan of action showing how expected results will be accomplished.

- Make sure that the person has the authority needed to carry out all parts of the delegated assignment.

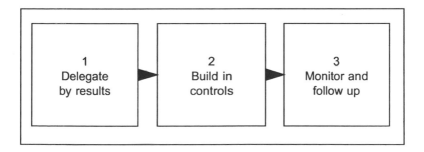

Fig. 16. Delegation grid.

And then – don't interfere. From that point on, the other person carries the ball. Too many managers delegate in theory, but then start meddling – giving advice, asking about the finer details, offering suggestions. Nothing communicates more clearly we don't really have confidence in the employee's capacity to decide what has to be done and do it.

2. Building in controls
We have to let the person take the ball and run with it – but we also

need to accept and exercise our ultimate responsibility for the work that is done.

● Build in controls – action plans, deadlines, periodic progress reports, and so on.

● Arrange informal interim meetings for periodic discussion and evaluation of progress.

● Follow up on specific tasks to make sure that they have been done properly.

● Keep yourself available to lend assistance when necessary. Be prepared to step in if necessary.

● But – always – judge by *results*. Don't insist that people do things the way you would do them.

3. Monitoring and following up

Jennifer Adair, Customer Service Manager with a London-based tour operator, uses the Quality Assurance principle of *spot-checking* to monitor how a delegated project is being carried out:

'When I've delegated something, I do spot-checks on how the person is doing. I pick one or two specific aspects of the project and ask some very explicit questions that require a fairly detailed response. That allows me to really get a sense of whether the person is on top of things. If his or her answer is convincing, then I can rest easy and assume that the project as a whole is in good hands and coming along nicely.'

On the subject of delegation, Jack had this advice:

'If you're going to check something, check it early on in the process. Review a rough draft of a report, for example, rather than waiting until the other person has spent a lot of time putting it into final form and polishing off all the rough edges. That way, there's less re-work needed. Try to approve what the person *plans* to do, and the thinking behind that plan, rather than the execution.'

Monitoring and following up isn't meddling. It's the logical, essential, and perfectly legitimate other side of the delegation coin.

MAXIMISING YOUR CHANCES

When you put forth a proposed solution to a problem you are usually competing for scarce resources. Constraints in terms of time, money, equipment and people mean that choices have to be made. And you want those choices to be made in your favour. Here are just a few guidelines to help.

Focusing on today's priorities, not yesterday's

If you were given a golden opportunity to solve a problem two months ago you should make sure that what was a high priority two months ago is still a high priority.

When someone hands us an invitation to take an in-depth look at what appears to be a high-priority issue – 'in-depth' meaning that it's going to take a month or more – it is imperative that we take a look, almost *daily*, to make sure that the issue hasn't shifted in some subtle way and that its priority hasn't changed.

Getting the key people involved

Anyone whose enthusiastic and diligent execution is crucial to success should be involved as early on and as extensively as possible.

Polishing your presentation skills

The ability to give a positive presentation is something that has to be *learned* and what makes a presentation successful is some disciplined attention – beforehand – to some very practical tasks:

- Find out who exactly will be at the meeting and what role they play in the decision-making process.

- Decide upon your goal for the meeting.

- Decide, if you can, what each of the people on the *other* side of the table will want to come away with.

- Think through the key concepts which you will need to implant in the audience's mind.

- Think through and prepare for the concerns, queries, or challenges which you might need to deal with.

- Think through people's current perceptions in regard to the actions that you want them to take.

- Identify what they will need to learn in order to accept the ideas that will be recommended.

- Identify the 'style' of communication that will best allow these ends to be achieved.

MAKING THINGS HAPPEN

Things don't happen unless someone makes them happen. In today's fast-moving business climate that statement probably represents the rule rather than the exception. Someone has to *drive* the process. If it's your problem, if it's your solution, then you're the one who has to make things happen.

ASSESSING RESULTS

Has the solution done its job? Has the problem been solved? By asking ourselves these questions we are effectively turning to the problem awareness step and seeing whether we still have a problem left to solve. If we do, we go on to Step Two again and gather facts about the new situation. If we don't then we call the whole process to a halt and look at things again in a week's time.

LEARNING FROM OUR SOLUTIONS

With hindsight, did we solve the problem in the most efficient and effective way possible? It is well worth asking this question and taking time to answer it properly.

Jack Carter again:

'One of the things that really impresses me about top performers is that they are always questioning themselves and scrutinising their own performance. It's probably the single most consistent thing that sets them apart from average people. They actually take time to sit down and *think* about themselves. And they want feedback; they'll lap up whatever feedback you can give them.'

Problem-solving, like any other skill, is something we *should* get better at as we go along.

KEY POINTS

- Work through the details. If something goes wrong, it will almost always be because of a detail.

- Build a visual plan if the solution is a 'project' involving several people or several steps.

- Get the right people involved – the people whose commitment will drive the process.

- Never underestimate the ease with which good ideas get sidetracked because of lack of commitment.

- Keep things simple. Kill one bird with many stones rather than two birds with one stone.

- Don't rely on good ideas to sell themselves. Get out there and personally sell the solution.

- Delegate ruthlessly at the implementation stage, but keep control of the process in your hands.

- If you are like most people, your presentation skills will not do justice to the quality of your ideas.

- Accept that no one cares about your solution as much as you do. Get out there and make it happen!

8
Creativity

The ability to 'come up with something' when something is needed... that's what we're going to work on in this chapter.

INTRODUCING TWO FORMS OF CREATIVITY

In practice, creativity seems to come in two main forms:

- In a situation where there is no routine solution to the problem, no precedent or policy to fall back on, the creative person comes up with an effective response.

- In a situation where there *is* a routine or standard solution the creative person comes up with something *new and better*.

In the first instance, the average person doesn't know what to do. The creative person thinks of something. In the second instance, the average person will do what has worked in the past. The creative person will look for something that's new and different.

Analytical barriers to creativity
The first step in tapping our creative ability is to clear away the blinkers which tend to inhibit creativity.

- *Overreliance on logic and precision.* It starts at school. We learn to equate logical reasoning with 'thinking' in general.

- *Black-and-white thinking.* The human brain has a neat way of simplifying things. In a grey world, our brain eases 'cognitive strain' by translating things into black and white whenever it can.

Emotional barriers to creativity
Emotional barriers and hang-ups can dampen creativity.

- *Fear of ridicule*: Stick with the tried and true. See what other people are thinking before you put your own thoughts on the table.

- *Failure to aim high*: Settling for a satisfactory result by borrowing from what we did last week or last month.

FINDING THE CREATIVE SOLUTION

We're struggling to solve a problem. We're going to have to *come up with something*.

Let's look briefly at some ways in which we can come up with something when we need to.

Visualising the end result
This is what Mozart had to say about the writing of his *Andante* of the Piano Concerto No. 21 in C.

'First bits and crumbs of the piece come and gradually join together in my mind; then the soul getting warmed to the work, the thing grows more and more, and I spread it out broader and clearer, and at last it gets almost finished in my head, even when it is a long piece, so that I can see the whole of it at a single glance in my mind, as if it were a beautiful painting or a handsome human being.'

This is a good example of someone *imagining* the end result before it has actually been created.

We can train ourselves. Just doing it – and getting better with practice. Try this:

- Sit back. Relax. Close your eyes. Loosen your shoulders. Take a deep breath, and let it out slowly. Now...imagine yourself having solved the problem. Develop the scene in your mind, as if you were watching it on video. You're relaxed; the tension is gone; the problem has been solved; the solution works; you're happy with it.

If Jack Nicklaus can visualise a golf ball dropping into a small hole in the ground 280 yards away – and then *do* it – then surely we can do the same sort of thing with our tasks and problems.

Thinking backwards
Start with the end result and work backwards. Visualise, in your

mind, the problem solved.

Imagine our problem is to reduce turnover on the sales team. We could pay them more money but let's try a different approach. Let's simply close our eyes and develop a mental image of the way things might be once our problem has been solved.

- It's a year from now. Whatever our turnover rate is it's not hitting us where it hurts. Most of the people who leave us are people we can afford to lose. Our top people are happy, and that's the main thing. Why? Because they are treated like senior professionals. Whether their long-term goal is to move into a Director of Sales & Marketing slot or be a consultant or run their own business, there's no better training ground in the world than what they have right now.

There's nothing magic here. We're simply describing a future state of affairs as if it existed right now.

Now...how did we get there? What did we do or say that led to that state of affairs?

Talking it through

If the essence of creativity is the ability to come at something from a whole new angle, then it makes sense to assume that a colleague is more likely to do that than *you* are. That's because they will come at it with an uncluttered mind. You won't.

And they can only do that if you bounce your ideas off them and get their reaction.

The other thing about talking something through is that it forces us to be precise. This is perhaps the single most powerful problem-solving tool of all. It *forces* us to be clear-headed.

Taking a long walk

Put your coat on and go for a walk.

Divide your walk into two parts. During the first part, concentrate on deep breathing from the diaphragm. If thoughts come into your mind just let them drift away. Focus on the breathing.

During the second part of your walk, shift your focus to the problem you've been wrestling with. You've given your brain some breathing space.

It's the release of tension – the relaxation – that is the secret. Tension and creativity are like chalk and cheese. To get your creative juices flowing, you need to get yourself into a relaxed frame of mind.

Drawing a picture of the problem

Sketch it out using boxes, circles and arrows, a bit like a flow chart. Use words as labels where appropriate but try not to write any elaborate **text**. Stick to pictures.

Drawing a picture is a very important aid to creativity:

- It allows events or items to be shown visually. Words – text – are a *linear* medium, unsuited to expressing things pictorially.

- Visual representation allows a great deal of information and ideas to be captured on a single page.

- It cuts down on the amount of information we need.

- We can keep related ideas and facts together.

Playing around with ideas

Play with them. Turn them over in your mind. Sleep on them. Talk about them over lunch with a friend or colleague. Tell your dog about them. Toy with the idea.

- I wonder what would happen if...?

- Wouldn't it be fun to try...?

- Has anyone ever tried...?

- I know this sounds far-out, but could we try...?

Thinking positively

One of the reasons some people don't spend enough time *toying* with ideas is that they are too quick to reject an unusual idea as not worth toying with.

As managers we must listen to suggestions with an open mind, try to appreciate the good points, and look for something to build upon.

That's the sort of attitude that encourages people to come forward with ideas.

Sleeping on it

As a last resort, put the whole thing aside and come back to it tomorrow. Worrying about it won't produce any useful result.

And *not* worrying about it *will*.

The technique is generally called **incubation** and it is generally assumed that our subconscious needs a chance to 'chew' on things and point us in the right direction.

Not always. But sleeping allows you to come back to the very same point the next day with a more relaxed mind and an invigorated spirit.

Doing a lot of reading

It is well established that both successful executives and creative thinkers tend to be voracious readers.

The debonair and well-read Tony Martindale, one or our *Famous Five*, had this to say:

> 'I remember being told that studying Latin was good for people because it was a way of exercising the brain, in much the same way that we exercise other parts of our body. At some level, I suppose I've never quite left that belief behind. The reason I enjoy a good game of chess, or a trip to the Tate Gallery, is because it activates and expands and challenges my mind. In some way or another, and it's not crucial that I know exactly how this happens, it makes my mind stronger.'

Both successful executives and creative thinkers are able to draw upon a storehouse of knowledge which allows them to bring in valuable insights which the more pedestrian thinker is unable to match.

Giving the problem to someone creative

It's always good to have at least one friend or colleague who has a distinctly 'creative' way of looking at things. They sometimes say things in meetings that seem childishly naïve but they come at things from a different angle.

ENCOURAGING CREATIVITY IN OTHERS

One of the real hallmarks of a successful manager is their ability to draw out creative thinking and problem-solving from other people.

Asking a question

A question that really causes people to have to *think* about what they are doing.

- Sounds good, Maggie. But just before we move ahead, let's ask ourselves . . . Can it be done better? This is good, but is there any way we can improve on it?

Looking at something from a variety of different points of view is one of the most critical ingredients of the creative process. And the asking of **questions** is the most obvious route to generating multiple perspectives.

Listening

Let the other person talk. Focus on understanding and fully *appreciating* what the person is saying. Speak only when a word or two of encouragement is needed to get the person to develop it further. Often, all that's needed is a slight nod of the head – anything that says that we're mentally working on what we have heard and would like to hear more.

Acknowledging an idea's merit

The key thing is to be open-minded, non-judgmental and *positive*. Even if the idea is far-fetched. What we *shouldn't* do is dismiss it out of hand.

- Ummm, that's an interesting idea, Frances. I'm not sure the committee would buy it, but if we could somehow shift the emphasis a bit from . . .

Putting a creative idea forward always involves a bit of a risk. And we want people to *take* that risk.

Don't focus on the details

When someone puts an idea forward, don't pick away at the details. Focus instead on the *gist* of the idea, on the essential thrust of the proposal. The details can be dealt with later.

Show enthusiasm

A manager can add value to the problem-solving process by expressing enthusiasm for an idea.

That sounds great, Bill! – will mean much more to Bill than you can possibly imagine. Your enthusiastic reception will allow him to unleash his own enthusiasm, and – most importantly – get his mental juices flowing.

KEY POINTS

- In a situation where there is no routine or standard solution to the problem, the creative person comes up with an effective response.

- In a situation where there *is* a routine or standard solution to the problem, the creative person comes up with something new and better.

- The capacity to visualise the end result seems to play some sort of central role in the creative process. It is something we can learn to do.

- Indeed, we can go a step further. We can visualise the end result – and then work backwards through time to see how we got there.

- Talking to people is one of the most useful things we can do. It gives us an excuse to verbalise our thoughts. It forces us to be clear-headed.

- Plus, other people are more likely than we are to come at a problem with an uncluttered mind. But they can only respond if you talk to them and bounce ideas off them.

- Actually get out of the building. Put your coat on and go for a walk. Go and spend some time in the open air.

- Tension and creativity are like chalk and cheese. To get your creative juices flowing, you need to get yourself into a relaxed frame of mind.

- Play around with ideas. Turn them over in your mind. Sleep on them. Talk about them over lunch. Tell your dog about them.

- Even if an idea seems far-fetched, don't dismiss it out of hand. Try to appreciate its good points. Look for something to build upon.

9
Intuition

In this chapter, we're going to take a more detailed look at **intuitive thinking** and put it to fruitful use at all stages in the problem-solving cycle.

Successful managers rely a great deal on intuitive thinking as a problem-solving tool. They do so effectively, not as an *alternative* to a more systematic or logical approach, but as a complement to it.

INTUITION AT WORK

Daniel Isenberg reported on two years of observational work with a dozen senior American managers.

'They seldom think in ways that one might simplistically view as "rational", i.e., they rarely systematically formulate goals, assess their worth, evaluate the probabilities of alternative ways of reaching them, and choose the path that maximises expected return. Rather, managers frequently bypass rigorous, analytical planning altogether, particularly when they face difficult, novel, or extremely entangled decisions. When they do use analysis for a prolonged time, it is always in conjunction with intuition.' ('How Senior Managers Think', *Harvard Business Review*, December, 1984).

Intuition seems to enter into the manager's day-to-day problem-solving activity in a number of ways:

- Intuition allows a manager to sense when a problem exists or is about to emerge.

- Intuition is what allows a manager to perform a routine task quickly and without thinking.

- It is quite common for managers to use intuition as a check on the results of data and analysis.

'By now it should be clear that intuition is not the opposite of rationality, nor is it a random process of guessing. Rather, it is based on extensive experience both in analysis and problem solving and in implementation, and to the extent that the lessons of experience are logical and well-founded, then so is the intuition. Further, managers often combine gut feel with systematic analysis, qualified data, and thoughtfulness.

It should also be clear that executives use intuition during all phases of the problem-solving process: problem finding, problem defining, generating and choosing a solution, and implementing the solution. In fact, senior managers often ignore the implied linear progression of the rational decision-making model and jump opportunistically from phase to phase, allowing implementation concerns to affect the problem definition and perhaps even to limit the range of solutions engendered.' (Ibid.)

UNDERSTANDING INTUITION

Intuition, rather than being an alternative to a more disciplined or rigorous mode of thinking, is actually a complement to it. The two work together as allies.

Over the years a manager might have worked systematically through enough problems to be in a position now to *sense* what's happening or about to happen.

The idea that our brain stores information about its successes and failures and then uses that information to generate solutions to problems is certainly not far-fetched. Most of us have had experiences where the answer to a problem has spontaneously come into our mind where we knew, *instinctively*, that this particular idea was good or that particular option would be ill-advised.

CONSIDERING WHEN INTUITION IS HELPFUL

Intuition has become an increasingly respectable and even *valued* commodity. True, managers are still trained, groomed and evaluated along rational lines, but intuition is no longer seen as something *alien* that should be excluded from the manager's intellectual tool kit.

Here are just a few examples where it becomes an essential part of the problem-solving process:

• Hard facts are few and far between, but the situation still demands a decision.

- The facts are there but they don't tell us what to do.

- Time is a factor. Extensive fact-gathering and analysis simply isn't going to be possible.

- There are several feasible solutions. A judgement call is required.

Note that these are all *decision-making* situations. Intuition comes into play most significantly in the decision-making stages of the problem-solving cycle.

But intuition also plays an important part at other stages in the cycle. At the initial **problem awareness** stage effective managers make liberal use of their intuitive powers to sniff out potential problems. During the **information gathering** and **problem definition** stages of the cycle their intuition allows them to develop a *feel* for how people are reacting and to develop a cognitive map of the total situation that they are dealing with.

So intuition is a well-nigh essential problem-solving tool. And that raises the question. *Can intuition be developed?*

LOOKING AT EVERYDAY INTUITION

Most of us rely quite heavily on intuition when reaching a decision. Through some sort of deductive process we know enough to search through only a limited number of possibilities.

Beyond that, however, how do we decide which decision is best? By and large, it's a matter of 'gut feeling'. When buying clothes, for example, we look at ourselves in the mirror. We look, in effect, at the whole person. And we either like what we see or we don't.

In everyday situations like this here's what seems to be happening:

- We look at the situation *visually* – not logically. We actually *look* rather than *analyse* or *think*.

- We look at ourselves, in the new dress or suit, in a full-length mirror.

- We develop an overall sense of whether there's a good fit or a bad fit, a 'right' or a 'wrong'.

DEVELOPING INTUITION

Intuition, then, is something that all of us use and experience in a wide range of everyday situations. Can we learn to apply this same process to work-related situations and problems?

1. Relaxing the thinking process

To allow intuitive data to come to the surface, you have to turn off the conscious 'thinking' part of your brain.

In other words, stop *thinking* about the problem. Take a break. Put the problem away and turn your attention to something altogether different.

2. Listening to your inner voice

Each of us has a little voice inside us.

It can act as a conscience telling us whether we've done good or bad. It nags away at us until we take action.

At other times, intuition takes the form of a *leaning* – that's the way it feels... we're *leaning* this way or that – toward a specific option in a decision-making situation.

Or it's not so much a leaning as it is a warning signal, a red flag, a vague feeling of discomfort.

3. Trusting your intuition

Too often, we tell the people around us *I had a* hunch *that would happen!* If that was the case, why didn't we speak up *before* the event?

Because we were afraid of being wrong. Not quite willing to really *trust* our intuition.

Or, in some cases, we trusted our intuition but would have been hard-pressed to defend it logically.

You: Hold on, Linda, that's not going to work, I just know it.
Linda: Why's that?
You: I don't know... I've just got a gut feel that we're doing this the wrong way...

Not a very compelling argument, is it?

4. Translating the intuition into action terms

If you announce that your instincts are telling you that an option is bad they're going to ask you *why*. They're going to ask you to translate your intuition into logical, factual, rational terms. It is much better to phrase your intuitive comment so that it refers to an action:

- Something tells me that this might be a good place to stop and take a breather.

- My instincts are telling me that we're moving too quickly here, that we've overlooked something.

The first statement refers quite explicitly to an action. The second does so in a more *implicit* fashion. Whether the reference is explicit or implicit, however, the result is the same; it invites people to say either 'Yes, you may be right' or 'No, I don't agree with you' – and then to share their own thoughts about the matter.

KEY POINTS

- Studies show that managers make generous use of intuition as a problem-solving tool – not as an alternative to rationality but as a complement to it.

- Intuition allows a manager to sense when a problem exisits or is about to emerge.

- Intuition allows a manager to perform a routine task – quickly and without thinking.

- It is quite common for managers to bring intuition in as a check on the results of a more systematic or rational analysis.

- Our subconcious mind will continue to work on a problem long after we have turned our conscious attention to something else.

- Intuition plays an important role throughout the entire problem-solving cycle – not just at the point where we actually make a decision.

- Intuition does not require special training or powers. Most of us rely quite heavily on intuition in every day situations.

- The key to developing intuition is to relax, listen to your inner voice, and trust what that voice is telling you when it makes its presence felt.

10
Strategic Thinking

Solving problems is one of those very basic managerial competencies that a good manager ought to know about.

Problem-solving in today's increasingly complex business environment also requires **strategic thinking**. Effective problem-solving involves:

- Dealing with complexity.
- Dealing with ambiguity.
- Seeing the real issues.
- Seeing the forest through the trees.
- Going to the heart of the matter.
- Seeing the big picture.

Jennifer Adair, Customer Service Manager with a well-known tour operator and one of our *Famous Five*, recognises the importance of strategic thinking – the capacity to move deftly between the macro and the micro view of things.

> 'One of the things I want our customer service people to be doing is thinking strategically and taking a strategic approach to solving customer problems. What that means is thinking about the problem behind the problem – and trying not just to solve the immediate problem at hand but also to address the larger issue which lies behind it.'

Tony Martindale, another of our *Famous Five* and the director of Sales and Marketing for one of the country's most dynamic packaged foods companies, is also aware of the importance of being 'strategic'.

'Rather than just moving into action, I think people have to stop and think through what sort of approach – on a more general level – is going to maximise their business results. You can't just go in there and sell, sell, sell any more. You have to know how you want to position yourself – and that means that you have to understand the things that drive the customer's business.'

The problem is that it is very difficult to define. No one seems to be quite sure exactly what it is, and that makes it difficult to describe how to *do* it.

> • An ageing Muhammed Ali resorted to his infamous *rope-a-dope* strategy to defeat George Foreman in the much celebrated heavyweight championship bout in Zaire – a strategy totally unlike the quick-footed brashness seen in the young Cassius Clay's thrashing of the moribund Sonny Liston. Ali and his handlers knew that the *Ali Shuffle* wouldn't have worked. The *rope-a-dope strategy* did.
>
> • Almost every week, it seems there is a new strategic link being forged between Tesco and a major name from outside the food retailing business – banking, dry cleaning, photography, insurance, clothing. Tesco's strategy for building competitive advantage, clearly, involves its being much more than just a *food* retailer.

A QUESTION OF STRATEGY

• What approach should we take?

• How should we come at this?

• How should we be trying to position ourselves?

• What's the best overall way to do this?

A **strategy** is a *way* of tackling a problem or working toward an objective.

• Our objective is to get our line of children's clothes being sold through *Safeway*. Our strategy is to demonstrate to the people at Safeway that we will work with them, as *partners*, to attract more customers into their stores.

What we are doing is plotting a *general approach* that will colour and shape and guide the more specific actions which will come into play as we work our way toward solving the problem or achieving our objective.

Let's go back to the case study in Chapter 4 which dealt with the problem of lagging sales. Tony was working behind the scenes on this one.

STEP 1 – STOP AND THINK

'Back in the old days, when sales were falling off a bit, you used to just crack the whip. In effect, you pushed the pressure down the ladder – 'Start hustling, you guys... get out there and sell!' This time around, however, I think we sensed that we were dealing with a problem that was going to require more than just a let's-get-out-there-and-work-harder sort of response.'

In other words, let's *not* just re-double our effort or push the pressure down the ladder or tell our people to get out there and work harder. Let's **stop and think** about this.

What we have to do, if we're going to think strategically, is shift the focus from action to *understanding*. Action will come later.

STEP 2 – STAND BACK

It's one thing to stop and think – but what do we think *about*? The secret, according to Customer Service Manager Jennifer Adair, is to discern the *patterns* in the problems which are coming to our attention.

'If a single customer calls in with a specific complaint, then we've got a one-off problem that we have to deal with. If three customers call in with the same complaint, then we have a *pattern*. That's when we have to start thinking strategically. There's something going on here, and we have to figure out what it is. Our top reps spot the patterns earlier – which is the key – and they can usually figure them out more quickly.'

In *every* problem-solving situation – 'strategic' or not – we feel we have to get down to the root causes.

When it comes to discerning patterns, however, the notion of unearthing the root problem doesn't quite fit. What's wrong is the language. It suggests that we bombard the problem with our *who-why-where-what-when* questions until we ferret out the underlying causes. In truth, however, thinking strategically seems to require an almost *opposite* sort of approach. The secret to seeing a pattern is to move back and view the immediate problem within its larger context.

If we do that we begin to see that the problem is part of a larger pattern. This is what we mean by seeing the problem in its total context. In the lagging sales case study in Chapter 4 the problem was defined in the following manner:

'Sales are down because our customers – schools, hospitals, and other institutions – are changing their buying habits. Their decisions are being driven increasingly by economic factors, and the decision-making process itself has become increasingly centralised. Buying groups have entered into the mix in a fairly significant way. In those accounts where we have a Key Account Management strategy in place, or where we have a strong performer with a 'consultative' approach to selling, we are doing okay. We are adapting to the changes. Across the board, however, sales are down. We need to take a long-hard look at how the industry is changing and at the implications thereof for our own approach to doing business.'

The problem is not just that sales are down. That is just a symptom. The real issue has to do with some fundamental questions of change, adaptation and strategy.

Notice how our definition of the problem now extends beyond the boundaries of our own organisation. It includes our customers, our competition, buying groups, legislative pressures, the industry as a whole. That's what happens when we stand back.

STEP 3 – RE-FRAME THE PROBLEM

When we stand back we move from the facts of the immediate situation to the *meaning* of those facts.

Step 3 involves thinking ahead to see how we can solve the problem.

Think ahead to see. This means that we play out, in our mind's eye, a successful resolution to the problem – keeping the total context in front of us.

'Once we had defined the problem in those terms, it became clear that we had to re-think our whole approach to the market. It's something we had been doing anyway, but not in any systematic way. What we realised is that we had to tighten up, and speed up, the process. Otherwise, we would get left behind by what was happening out in the marketplace.'

Notice how the original problem – lagging sales – has been reworked. We have re-framed the problem as one of developing a strategy consistent with the fundamental changes occurring in the marketplace.

'The message that we tried to put out was simple. Let's worry about developing a rock-solid relationship with our customer. Let's get to the point where we're helping them achieve their own strategic objectives, focus on identifying their needs and delivering solutions that meet those needs, then our 'sales' will take care of themselves.'

That meant not just a change in people's *thinking*, but some corresponding and supportive organisational changes as well. During the ensuing months, two important things were achieved.

'We developed a new account planning process that got us all thinking in terms of building strategic partnerships with our major customers. At the same time, we re-organised our sales organisation so that each of our top ten accounts now has an Account Executive heading up our account team and acting as the principal contact with the total account. So now – rather than a major hospital being called on by five different reps with five different product lines and five different sales plans – we have a single team headed up by a single person going in there with a single strategic plan.'

These are solutions which involve a change in a company's whole strategy as it takes its product to the marketplace – which in turn requires a fundamental shift in people's thinking backed up by some fairly significant changes of an organisational and structural nature. So – let's summarise.

● *Stop and think*: We resist the natural temptation to move into action. Instead, we stop and think.

● *Stand back*: Rather than *digging in* to the problem, we *stand back* and look at it within its total context.

- *Re-frame*: We re-frame the **Fix-It** problem as a **Do-It** problem, We turn it into a positive challenge.

EVERYDAY PROBLEMS

What about those of us who are not operating at the director level? Do we still have to worry about thinking 'strategically' over problems like this?

- Barbara is going to be late for the meeting.
- The people in Marketing don't understand the memo that we sent around.

These call for remedial action or no action at all. These are not *complex* problems.

Or is there more there than meets the eye?

Barbara may have a *habit* of being late, for example, or the misunderstood memo may signal a fundamental problem in communicating across departmental boundaries.

That's the first step in thinking strategically. Specifically, we assume that what we're seeing is not just a one-off problem; it is part of a *pattern*.

Let's take one of our problems – the people in Marketing don't understand the memo that we sent around – and expand upon the *pattern* which it might well represent.

If it turns out that we're not talking the same language – (marketing focuses on things like brand awareness while we look at things like inventory returns as being critical to the business) and each side doesn't understand the other's priorities, because we rarely sit down around the same table – then we have a pattern on our hands.

This is where we switch from thinking **Fix-It** to thinking **Do-It**. The solution isn't to rush out and explain the memo to them. We have to find ways to break down the barriers that exist between departments within this company.

BARRIERS TO STRATEGIC THINKING

In many cases, major corporations exercise strategy by default. IBM didn't consciously *choose* to remain big and almost fall by the wayside as smaller and more nimble competitors began to eat away at its core businesses.

No, they just kept on doing what they had always done in the same way that a person might go on acting like a couch potato long after the damage done to their health has become worrisomely apparent. It's not a conscious strategic choice. It's a *lack* thereof.

Success

Why change? We've always been successful doing things the way we do them.

Companies, of course, don't talk to themselves this way. No, the truth of the matter is that they don't talk to themselves at all. And that is precisely the problem. They operate on the basis of the above *assumptions*. By the time the problem announces itself in the form of lagging sales and poor year-end results the internal *causes* of the problem have generally reached a fairly advanced state.

Lack of success

Who has time to sit back and think about 'strategy'? All we can do is grab whatever business we can get.

During their early start-up years, many entrepreneurs make precisely the same mistake that IBM was guilty of. They operate on the basis of unconscious assumptions. By the time the *Strategy Vacuum* problem shows itself the internal functions are damaged almost beyond repair.

Lack of time

For *individuals* this is probably the number one barrier. That's what nine out of ten managers will tell you if you ask them why 'strategic' thinking is being squeezed out of their busy schedules.

It raises the question, of course, as to why those other things are considered to be more important than strategic thinking.

Crisis management

It is difficult to address the strategic issues if we spend most of our day putting out fires and dealing with minor crises.

'I get twenty telephone calls a day, and heaven knows how many faxes. Every one of them is an urgent problem that I have to deal with. It all gets dumped on my lap. And what's happened is that I've gotten trapped into this Fire-Fighting role to the point where that's how the customer sees me. I'm the guy that their store managers call when there's a delivery problem. And you wonder why my boss rates me as not being very good at "addressing the strategic issues in this account".'

The word *trapped* is a telling one. Crisis management drowns out strategic thinking thus reinforcing the need for more crisis management. And there are times when it seems that the only way to break out of this vicious cycle is to close the whole business down for a few days. But the world won't allow us to do that. So we struggle on.

Concrete thinking

Some people have difficulty thinking in the abstract. They can recount what happened in a movie but they have great difficulty summing it up in twenty-five words or less.

There seems to be a fairly tangible skill involved here. People who *have* it are good at summarising and giving you a brief overview in their own words.

People who *don't* have it tend to get bogged down in the details.

A skillful chess player has the skill. They are able to *sense* how the game is unfolding and what lies ahead.

Unconscious assumptions

The Body Shop company is experimenting with a new **strategy** that challenges the assumption that, in order to sell, women's bodycare products have to be 'glamorous'. The new Body Shop campaign, with its use of both realistic text and very realistic 'models', turns this whole assumption on its head.

The unconscious assumption that models have to be glamorous hinders strategic thinking. It lulls us into thinking that we needn't think strategically because there is only one strategy.

REMEDY NUMBER 1: ASKING THE RIGHT QUESTIONS

One of the real secrets is simply to ask oneself the right questions.

What is going on here?

Not *What do we do?* or even *What is wrong?* Moving ahead on the basis of unconscious assumptions is deadly and it is important that we avoid doing so right at the outset.

So we ask ourselves the most open-ended question *What is going on here?*

Is this part of a bigger problem?

Kevin's presentation to the people at GKN got, at best, a lukewarm response. We'll have to sit down with Kevin, look in some detail at how the presentation went, and figure out what we can do to get the proposal back on track.

But there's a 'pattern' issue. Doing presentations at the senior level is a vital part of Kevin's role and he is not terribly good at. He doesn't *engage* people's thinking, get them excited or bring his ideas to life.

REMEDY NUMBER 2: GETTING AWAY

Getting outside the work environment seems to help.

> 'My boss suggested that I take a couple of days off at Land's End and really *think* about what I wanted to achieve with the customer account. I didn't quite see how booking myself into a hotel at Land's End would solve the problem. With hindsight, however, it's one of the best things I've ever done.'

Getting away from it all was part of the solution. But an equally important part has to do with what you do when you are there.

> 'My boss suggested taking what he called a Back-from-the-Future approach. You think about where you'd like to be in, let's say, a year from now. And then you come back into the present and put together a plan that will take you there. In my case it meant creating an image in my mind of the way I would be operating the account a year from now. Who I would be spending time with, the role of the other people on the account team, the new products we'd be bringing out...everything.'

REMEDY NUMBER 3: THINKING BACKWARDS

This is an especially useful tool when the solution to our problem involves a person, group or organisation other than ourselves. The problem might be to get the sales people to give us more accurate forecasts, or encourage the people on our team to think more creatively about things. In both of these cases, the solution has to do with a reaction or behaviour that has to occur in *someone else*.

So we think backwards.

'Okay, I'm the hospital. I've decided to buy not just more sutures and drapes but a whole package of products cemented into a two-year contract. I did that because it lowered my costs. It reduced the number of orders that had to be processed and the number of decisions that had to be made.'

Now, as the vendor, *selling* these products into the hospital, what does this tell me about my strategy?

'We got their business because we positioned ourselves as a means of cutting their administrative costs.'

We got their business because we positioned ourselves as – is a very important first half of a *strategic* statement. If you complete it you are making a statement of strategy. Here are some other examples of strategic half-statements:

- 'We got their approval because we demonstrated that...'
- 'We convinced them by presenting our idea as ...'
- 'They bought the programme because they saw it as...'
- 'We sold the deal by positioning it as a solution to...'

Complete any of these statements and you end up with a way of *presenting* something that creates a favourable reaction or perception from the other party.

REMEDY NUMBER 4: THINKING PICTORIALLY

Returning to the notion of pictorial thinking under this new heading reinforces the close tie between creative and strategic thinking.

There's an example of pictorial thinking in Figure 17. Problem-solving, it says, can be thought of as a process comprised of six fundamental steps.

There are some really neat things about this diagram. It sums up in a few square inches what might take a whole *chapter* of text to properly describe. The diagram also captures the process, the movement of problem-solving. It's easy to remember. If we had to give a speech on problem-solving this diagram would serve our purpose much more effectively than anything we could find in textual form.

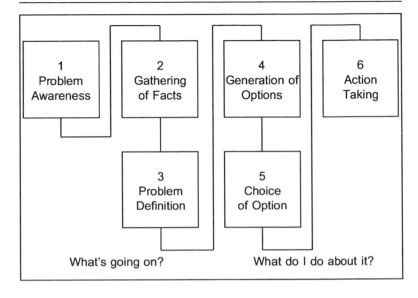

Fig. 17. Thinking pictorially.

REMEDY NUMBER 5: TALKING TO SOMEONE

It helps to talk.

- 'Talking with Tony allowed me to see it as an outsider would see it. To get a sense of perspective about the whole thing. To look at it from the standpoint of other people in the various departments under Tony.'

REMEDY NUMBER 6: EXPLAINING IT TO THE BANK MANAGER

As a last resort, take two simple steps.

1. Imagine that you own the company.

2. Imagine that you have to explain your strategy to your bank manager.

- 'This is the problem, this is why I think it's important, this is the strategy I've been using to tackle it, these are the options I've looked at, and this is where I am right now.'

KEY POINTS

- The concept of strategic thinking gets to the heart of what effective problem-solving – in today's complex business environment – is all about.

- A strategy isn't a goal or an action plan. It's an approach to something. It's a *way* of tackling a problem or working toward an objective.

- What we have to do, if we're going to think strategically, is shift the focus from action to understanding. We have to resist the urge to do something.

- The first step is to assume that things aren't quite as straightforward as they look – that the problem we're seeing is part of a larger pattern.

- Rather than digging into the problem, what we need to do is stand back from the problem – rise above it, view it from a more general plane.

- Then we re-frame the problem as a Do-It problem rather than a Fix-It problem. We shift from thinking reactively to thinking proactively.

- The need to deal reactively with the immediate problem gives way to an opportunity to tackle – proactively – a larger and more significant issue.

11
Selling the Solution

For some people, the notion of having to 'sell' their ideas sounds vaguely disreputable.

MAKING IT HAPPEN

Janet McIntyre, Human Resources Director of one of the UK's biggest ice cream producers:

> 'The single biggest stumbling block is the inability to sell internally. If you have to get something approved you have to know how decisions are made and who is involved. You have to make it happen. You have to be proactive.'

Proactive. It means managing the process.
There are also some important interpersonal **skills** involved here. Back to Janet McIntyre.

> 'You have to know how to approach people. They have their own schedules and their own priorities. You have to win people over. You have to show them the pay-off for helping out.'

MAPPING THE DECISION

If the implementation of your solution means a decision is needed by your superior then you have to take responsibility for managing the decision-making process as much as you possibly can. The most important step of all is to *understand* the total decision-making process.

- Who exactly will be involved in the making of the decision, and at what specific stage?

- What specific role will each person play in the total decision-making process?

- What will each person be looking for? What criteria will they apply to the decision?

- How do they perceive and/or feel about your proposed solution right now?

Decisions are rarely made by a single person. There is a cast of players and a process they follow which you have to *influence* in order that your proposed solution gets the commitment you are looking for.

What are each of these people looking for? What criteria will they use to assess and judge your proposed solution? What are the specific benefits or outcomes that they will need to see?

How are they reacting to it? Disinterested? Sceptical? Lukewarm? Interested? Enthused? At each point in the decision-making process, each of the key players will have a certain perception of your proposed solution and a certain reaction to it, and it would be ideal if we:

1. knew what that perception and reaction was, and

2. had a plan for moving it toward the enthusiastic end of the continuum.

These are tough questions, and tough challenges. You might have to talk directly to the key players on a one-to-one basis. At the very least, there are clearly some things here that you will have to think about.

All this can be thought of as charting the people and the process, and then keeping that chart up to date as it changes.

RESISTANCE TO CHANGE

There are times when the solution we have come up with is going to affect a large number of people. And it is on such occasions that we sometimes encounter a widespread resistance to anything that is new or at odds with the way things have been done for the last twenty years.

Let's examine, briefly, some of the myths that surround this whole issue of *resistance to change*.

People don't like new technology

That's nonsense, of course. The same people who resist the

introduction of new technology into the mail-sorting room are the same ones who line up to buy the latest hi-fi equipment and electronic toys at Curry's or Dixon's during the pre-Christmas rush.

A good idea will sell itself

Perhaps a good idea *should* sell itself. But it doesn't.

There are lots of good ideas around but none of these make much of a dent in our thinking or the way we do things. It is only when a specific idea can be related to a specific need being satisfied that we really pay attention to an idea.

And that's not something that can happen passively. It's the *selling* of the idea – one person's active relating of the idea to the specific need of the other person – that penetrates the barrier of disinterest.

There are times when *poorer* ideas are more apt to be adopted than *better* ideas. And that is because the person whose idea it is will put more work into packaging and selling it. People *think* about it. It engages their thinking. And it ends up being accepted. The superior idea, having been presented passively in the form of a proposal or report, sits untouched.

People read things we give them to read

People don't read outlines or manuals that we send around. Anything that's longer than a few lines is unlikely to be read by any more than two or three people out of twenty. Most people aren't 'readers' by nature.

So we can never assume that something has been read, or understood, just because it has been 'sent around'.

Resistance has to be 'overcome'

The very word 'resistance' has an adversarial colouring to it. It clearly implies that *we* – the good guys – are trying to move ahead with a solution and *they* – the bad guys – are an obstacle standing in our way. So part of our planning has to be a strategy for *overcoming* that resistance.

And, that, of course, is almost *asking* for trouble. At the very least, it sets up a self-fulfilling prophecy when we leave the other side out of the early discussions.

If there *is* resistance to change, then it is important that we look upon it as a signal that something about the whole change process needs a bit more care and attention.

GOING IN WELL-PREPARED

In many situations, the selling of a solution takes place in the form of a presentation. However it is done, the key thing is that you have time to think things through in advance, shape and fine-tune your arguments, and develop a convincing presentation.

Preparation means asking the right questions, and then doing the considerable mental homework needed to answer those questions comprehensively in advance.

What is needed?

If people are unclear about what the issue is and what your solution might be, then they will not be in a position to accept the rationale behind your solution. Never assume that people understand. Spell it out.

What has been tried before?

We need to have a thorough understanding of what has been done in the past and with what degree of success.

We have to show that we can address the issues promptly and smartly and demonstrate exactly how and why our proposed solution is better.

What are the other options?

We have to let people know that we have considered other options very carefully, weighed their respective merits, and settled on the one specific option that will best work in our favour.

What are others doing?

How are our competitors handling this problem? Baxter struggled with this issue for a whole year; what did *they* end up doing?

You have to have answers for these questions. Executives pay a lot of attention to what their competitors are doing. They keep their eyes, too, on what successful companies in other industries are doing. If someone else out there has found a solution to the problem, let's find out what they did. And then let's do it better.

How would we proceed?

What would the first step be? Who would be involved? How would the project be managed? How long would it take? How much would it cost?

At some point people are going to want answers to these

questions. You have to have the answers available and those answers have to specific and well thought out.

GETTING PEOPLE INVOLVED

Working colleagues all have their own busy schedules and their own priorities. And while yes, it's true that we all work for the same company, the fact is that we each have to keep our bosses happy. The priorities of someone in Accounting are never going to overlap with the priorities of someone in Sales or Marketing, and there is no point in beating people over the head with the old adage that we all have to do what's good for the customer.

No, the idea of their involvement is something that has to be *sold*. Here's how we can do it.

Acknowledging their priorities
- 'I know you've got a busy afternoon ahead of you, Frank, but I wonder if I can just get a couple of pieces of information from you.'

That's a good way of letting Frank know that *we* know he has lots of other things to do. It's a good example of taking the customer's most likely objection, voicing it before they have a chance to do so, and then sweeping it off the table.

Looking and sounding like a winner
People like to be associated with a winner.

If you sound like a non-winner with an apologetic tone to your voice and your whole manner is flat and devoid of enthusiasm then you're going to have to twist their arms if you hope to get them involved.

Be explicit about what you want – and why
- 'What I need is some marketing input. We need someone on the team who can relate what we're trying to do here to what's been done in the US – and I figure you're the ideal person to bring that kind of perspective to the table.'

Spell it out. And do it in a positive way that pinpoints the specific value that someone's presence will add to the team.

Spelling out the benefits

Think carefully about this beforehand. Think it through from the other person's vantage point. *What's in it for me?*

- 'This might be a good chance for you to see, Judy, how all this data you generate is being used at the sharp end of the business.'

- 'It'll be good exposure for you, Jack. Howard and Maureen are both going to be there, and they'll be paying particular attention to this issue.'

RIGHT FROM THE START

There's no point in spending hours and hours analysing a problem and developing a solution if it turns out that your superiors have already decided to move in a different direction putting your solution on hold until next year.

Nor do you want to propose a solution that goes against the grain of the board's thinking or that has no chance of gaining support because of its similarity to a proposal rejected last autumn.

We shouldn't look at 'selling the solution' at the tail-end of the problem-solving process. It is something you should be thinking about right from the start.

KEY POINTS

- Good ideas don't sell themselves. If our proposed solution needs to be vetted, it has to be good. It has to make sense. But it also has to be sold.

- No one cares as much about your proposed solution as you do. Another mantra that we should repeat to ourselves until we get sick of hearing it.

- You have to be proactive. You have to champion the solution and drive the total problem-solving process. You have to make it happen.

- Clear understanding of the total decision-making process will decide whether your solution is accepted or rejected.

- Who is involved? What role does each person play? What specific criteria will apply? How does each person perceive and feel about our proposal?

- You have to find answers to these questions, and take positive action to move the total process – and each key player – toward a favourable position.

- A single presentation can make or break our case. The key here is preparation – knowing what questions count, and having answers for them.

- We also have to know how to get individual people involved when needed. It helps, for one thing, to have a 'network' in place.

- Acknowledge their priorities. Recognise that people have their own concerns and their own busy schedules – and let them know that you recognise it.

- Look and sound like a winner. People enjoy being part of a success story. Don't sound apologetic or diffident when you ask for people's involvement.

- Be explicit about what you want – and why. Spell it out. Tell each person in a positive way what specific value he or she will add to the total effort.

- Spell out the benefits. What's in it for them? Put yourself in the other person's shoes. What exactly do they have to gain by getting involved?

- Don't leave it too late. If people's commitment or involvement is going to be crucial to getting your solution acted upon, get out there and start selling.

12
Managerial Problem-solving

This book is about *you* as a problem-solver. We also have to look at you as a *manager*. If you have people reporting to you on the organisation chart, then you are by definition a manager. That's the conventional definition. These days, however we are being paid to provide leadership, to facilitate, to assist...without having these people 'report' formally to us. So in view of this, you should consider yourself a **manager**.

There are certain aspects of the problem-solving cycle and strategy which need to be looked at from a **managerial** point of view. That is what we are going to do in this chapter.

THE CONCEPT OF LEVERAGE

Leverage – not the number of people reporting to you – is what defines a managerial role as 'managerial'.

Leverage is what you get when you use a pulley system to control the boom on a sailboat rather than a single rope. It multiplies the amount of *power* you can generate.

Leverage is what we as managers use to produce results which go far beyond anything we could produce acting entirely on our own. By training someone, by passing along skills, by developing tools which other people can use, we are exercising leverage.

As managers, leverage is what we have to aim for. In everything we do.

If, on the other hand, we say 'Move over, Jim, let me see if I can figure it out', then we're *not* exercising leverage. We're just operating as a single employee solving a single problem. We're standing in for Jim.

That might be valuable. It may allow an important problem to get solved. But it's not leverage.

Given the scarcity of time at our disposal and the increasing importance of getting things right...we can't, as managers, afford to do anything *less* than exercise leverage.

DIRECTING – THE NATURAL IMPULSE

Let's take some typical problems that might come to our attention as managers.

- One of your people has a crucial meeting tomorrow with a major supplier. You've asked him or her to come in and talk things over.

- One of your people has called *you* and asked for some time.

- A customer is furious, and is threatening to cancel an important programme. You're still not quite sure what's happened.

These are all important situations and action has to be taken. In most cases, time is of the essence.

The *old* way of managing is to step in and do people's thinking for them.

- 'Just get whatever you have out on the truck, Mark. There's no point in having it go out half-empty. The rest of the packing can wait.'

- 'I think what we need to do, Jill, is take a more aggressive approach. Let's let them know that we're sure of our ground and have no intention of backing off.'

These ways of reacting are things we do naturally and instinctively. We solve the problem for them.

We'll call this the **directive approach** to managing. It means that we are trying to be helpful by offering a solution to the problem.

There are, however, some pitfalls when we do this.

- *You have to be there.* If you're tied up in a meeting the problem isn't going to get solved.

- *No learning occurs.* No one learns much about the actual problem-solving process.

- *You may be wrong.* What looks right from your managerial perch may, when seen from ground level, not be the best solution at all.

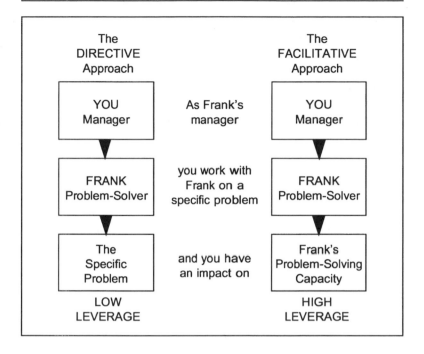

Fig. 18. Comparing the directive approach with the facilitative approach.

The big problem is the fact that no-one learns anything. In other words, there's no **leverage**. You haven't left the other person better equipped to solve the *next* problem or make the *next* decision.

FACILITATING – THE BETTER WAY

Let's compare the *directive* approach to managing with the **facilitative approach**. Figure 18 provides an illustration.

Frank comes to us with a problem, or a decision he has to make. He's not sure how to handle it.

We start with an important assumption. *Frank is capable of solving this problem. I don't have to solve it for him.*

But he does need help. He's capable of finding the solution, but he doesn't see it yet. He needs some help.

Still – the fact remains: Frank has to come up with the solution himself. People learn best, and solve problems best, when they arrive at the solution themselves. Our job, as managers, is to help them do that.

OUR VALUE-ADDED CONTRIBUTION

What we want to do is enhance Frank's solution of the problem. What is it, precisely, that we as managers bring to the process?

The wisdom of experience
We probably have more years under our belt. We know the system better.

* So we've probably encountered similar problems in the past. We've seen what works and what doesn't.

* We can add the sort of realism that comes with experience.

* We probably have a better sense of perspective and proportion.

A sounding board
We act as a sounding board. Frank will be able to talk things through rather than think things through.

* Having to put his thoughts into words forces him to be logical and coherent.

* Hearing them spoken aloud will give him a sense of objectivity. Nothing helps a person's thinking more than the need to put their thoughts into words.

Ideas and suggestions
Two heads are better than one. We can contribute to the problem-solving process. Background information, inside information, 'political' information, the sort of stuff that comes with our greater experience and knowledge of the 'system'.

Someone to argue with
Even if all we do is argue with Frank, at least we'll be forcing him to think through his ideas and find ways to rebut or refute our arguments. He'll come away better prepared for any adversarial encounters that might be awaiting him as he moves forward with his action plan.

THE MAGIC OF ASKING QUESTIONS

As a way of getting people to think along lines that we *know* will be productive... nothing is as powerful as asking a question.

What exactly are we trying to achieve here – is basically an invitation for the other person to *think*. But, used skilfully, it can do more than that. It can help us – as Frank's manager – to help *Frank* think:

- logically
- broadly
- incisively
- resourcefully
- creatively
- boldly
- realistically
- empathetically
- proactively
- decisively.

Let's look at how it's done.

1. Logically
This is one of two fundamental dimensions that add value to Frank's thinking:

- thinking horizontally
- thinking broadly.

First, the **horizontal**. We want him to *think* about cause-and-effect. What leads to what? We want him to think **logically**. If I do this, then that will happen, and that in turn will cause this to happen, at which point I will...

- 'Okay, if we do that, what is his reaction likely to be? Try to put yourself in his shoes...'

- Or, 'Okay, Frank, but let's think about that a bit. You do this or that. What's going to happen then?'

You may have to bring in *your* experience and insights if he thinks through cause-effect relationships and doesn't see an outcome that you know is there.

First, though, try to get *him* to see it.

- 'Okay, Frank, that's his reaction on day 1. Think for a minute about day 2. He's back in his office, and he't got his calculator out and he's adding up the figures...'

You're asking an explicit question. You're pointing his gaze into a specific area that he hasn't yet examined. Your helpfulness, your value added, stems from the simple fact of *directing* his thinking.

2. Broadly

Here, our aim is to help Frank stand back and take an overview of the situation as it might be *at any one point in time*.

We want Frank to see himself as but one piece in a large puzzle. We want him to see how things in one part of the overall system will have an impact on other parts.

- 'Okay, Frank, but let's look at the other players involved. What's their stake in all this, and how are they likely to react?'

One of the most difficult things for a subordinate to do is to look at all sides of a problem or issue with objectivity. The closer we are to a situation, the less likely we are to see all sides of it.

As managers, we can bring a sense of perspective to bear but we have to remain in our managerial role. If we become too deeply involved then the advantages of our broader perspective can easily be dissipated.

3. Incisively

One of the most useful things we can do is help people get down to the essentials.

- 'Jack, you've given me three pages with lots and lots of words. What we need is a one-page list of numbers that shows how we're adding dollars to the customer's bottom line.'

There's a danger of failing to define the problem properly and we end up not coming to grips with the real and more basic issue.

- 'Okay, Frank. Let's take a deep breath and see if we can't make sense of this whole situation. What's the single most important element that we have to pay attention to?'

Let's take a deep breath. This suggests standing back, looking at the whole thing. And once he's done that he has to answer a specific question. *What's the real issue here?*

4. Resourcefully

What does Frank need to learn or get from other people? Whose help and support will he need? How can he marshal his resources in such a way as to *maximise* their impact?

Our aim here – and again, we achieve it primarily through asking questions – is to encourage Frank to make full use of the resources which we, as a company, can offer.

- 'Frank. Are you the person who should be dealing with this problem? And, if you are, are there other people you need to get involved?

5. Creatively

- 'I think your idea is sound, Frank. Are there any other approaches we might want to consider?'

Here, we're encouraging Frank to think of something new and different.

- 'How about..?'

- 'What about..?'

- 'Have you thought about..?'

- 'What would happen if..?'

We're putting specific action options forward in a gentle, but questioning form.

Try this on (Action) and see where it leads you (Outcomes). Look at the outcomes that this action would produce.

Notice that we don't just say *I think you should* do this. Why not? For one thing, there may be a practical flaw in the idea that we are not aware of but that he will see from his ground-level perspective.

Most importantly, he has to make it his own idea in order for it to work. We don't want him mechanically executing an action that we have prescribed. He will have to do it at the most favourable time and in the appropriate manner. It can't be *programmed*. It has to come from him.

6. Boldly

Our focus here is on helping Frank weigh the dangers and payoffs inherent in a course of action. If we sense he's confining his thinking to low-risk options, we might encourage him to examine bolder strategies. Or, if he is already thinking along risk-laden lines, we'll want to make sure that he has weighed the pros and cons.

- 'I wonder if that's as risky as it sounds, Frank. Let's think it through...'

7. Realistically

We want Frank to think about what's possible and what's not, about how much support or co-operation he will get from people, about how long things will take. We want him to assume that, as a rule, things take a lot longer than one might reasonably expect.

- 'You're assuming that these guys are going to go along with you, but I wonder...Will they? What have we seen in the past?'

8. Empathetically

We want Frank to be aware of the customer's priorities, needs and concerns. And this applies both to a customer who buys our products or an *internal* customer.

- 'Put yourself in the customer's shoes, Frank. What's important to you? What are you worried about? What do you need to see? What do you need to hear?'

9. Proactively

We want Frank to be always looking for ways to make things happen, to keep the ball in his court...

- What can we do?
- Where's our leverage?
- How can we keep the ball rolling?
- How can we make it happen?
- How can we steer the course of events?
- How can we influence what he thinks or does?
- How can we prevent that from happening?

Again, the trick for you as a manager isn't to have *answers* to these questions. It's to *ask* them.

10. Decisively

We want Frank to have a little voice in the back of his mind always asking *What are you going to do and when are you going to do it?*

It's a challenging question. Asking it is one of the most useful things we can do as managers.

LOOKING FOR LEVERAGE

Our biggest challenge as managers is to find and exercise every ounce of **leverage** that we possibly can.

Investing in time

Time – or, more to the point, a *lack* of time – is something that we would do well to keep reminding ourselves of again and again as we work through the average week.

Jennifer Adair, one of our *Famous Five*, had this to say:

'I think of my time as being 'invested' in things. So I'm always asking myself – Is this a good investment? Is there a significant benefit to be gained here? How large is the payoff compared to what it would be if I did this... or this... or this? I don't spend a lot of time exploring these issues; it's more like a quick computation that I do in my head, automatically, every time I have to choose what to do next.'

Too often, we're reacting to events as they unfold. We're being *reactive* rather than *proactive*. We're not making conscious decisions.

The challenge is to bring our *usage* of time under our direct and conscious control by making conscious, intelligent decisions.

Keeping informed

Getting *good* information is always a challenge. There are going to be some people whose opinions you can count on but it's best to assume that others will be somewhat self-serving in how they convey information and opinion to you.

We need to cultivate our sources and take a discerning approach to assessing what we hear from them.

Tony Martindale:

'I always know that with Andrea (Tony's Human Resources director), I'll always get an honest – sometimes brutally honest – appraisal of things. And that's something I appreciate. If I need to bounce an idea around, or discuss something off the record, or think out loud about a very difficult decision involving someone on staff, I always know I can do it with Andrea. She's a great sounding board, and she's not afraid to pull me up if I'm waffling or not making any sense.'

Reserving time for 'walking around'
Don't allow all of your time to get tied up with meetings, luncheons, and the like. You should reserve a chunk of time every day for 'managing by walking around'.

It's your only opportunity to get a *feel* for what is happening and – importantly – to give people a chance to come to you with information or problems that they feel are important.

Moving in and out of situations
As we're 'managing by walking around', we come across some juicy, here-and-now problems that are very enticing. And it is difficult to know whether to plunge in with both feet, studiously avoid getting involved, or seek out the middle ground.

Getting the balance right is tricky. If you have ever watched a good primary school teacher you will have seen how it ought to be done. No, you don't plunge in with both feet. You stop at this table just long enough to lavish praise before going on to the next table to sort out a scrap and then you glance around the room before wandering over to the table where Jeremy and Paul have just managed to spill a can of paste.

This is multi-tasking at its most demanding and it represents a pattern of managerial behaviour which most of us should be striving to emulate. A nudge here. A word of advice there. Good managers linger just long enough to make a *difference*. And then they keep moving.

Linking the specific to the general
When senior managers talk about problems, they often shift between the specific and the general.

'Jim is after me to set up a committee to look at whether we belong in the home care market. That's the kind of decision we don't seem to make very well around here. We're superb on the operational stuff; but when it comes to the directional issues, the wheels seem to spin forever unless I step in.'

There's a specific issue that has to be resolved, having to do with the home care market. And it looks as if our unnamed executive will be involved, albeit grudgingly, in making that decision. Of equal interest, though, is the telling comment – *That's the kind of decision we don't seem to make very well around here.* That observation has to do with *process.* It has to do with a trend of which the home care issue is but a single symptom.

This is a sophisticated form of leverage which we find in experienced senior managers. They think about problems on two different levels.

> **That's the sort of thinking that a high-leverage manager has to be doing all the time... reserving their attention for those higher-level issues which cut across divisions and departments and functions.**

CONVERTING PROBLEMS INTO OPPORTUNITIES

Good managers have a way of converting **problems** into **opportunities**.

Calling it an opportunity doesn't mean that we've solved the problem or make it any *easier* to solve the problem. What it does, though, is put a positive face on it.

> **What we've effectively done is taken a *Fix-It* type of problem and bolted a *Do-It* problem onto it.**

It also makes a problem worth solving – if there was any doubt about that in the first place. You're not just dealing with a specific incident. You're building a more effective, more prosperous organisation by putting a better procedure in place or by changing the way people *think* about an issue.

Challenging others to do likewise

'Linda, we've had a number of complaints from customers over the past three months about products being shipped a day or two late. I'd like you to look into it and see what the problem is and what we can do about it.'

That's straightforward enough. Linda, here's a practical problem which is important. Find out what's causing it and do whatever has to be done to make it go away.

Imagine how much more exciting it would be to add on the following:

> 'Linda, I want our level of service to be a key selling feature all by itself. I want customers to absolutely *rave* about the way we treat them. Clearly, on the basis of what I've been hearing, we're not there yet. I'd like you to put together a strategy for making this a truly customer-driven organisation.'

Not just 'solve this problem'... but *use* this problem.

KEY POINTS

- If the whole thrust of your job is to have an impact on the way things are done by other people around you, then you are a 'manager'.

- Leverage allows us to wield an influence that extends farther and deeper than anything we could produce if we were acting on our own.

- As managers, leverage is what we have to aim for. In everything we do. We can't afford to do anything *less* than exercise leverage.

- The directive approach to management involves trying to be helpful by offering a solution to the problem – giving advice, for example.

- People learn best, and solve problems best, when they arrive at the solution themselves. Our job, as managers, is to help them do that.

- The facilitative approach to managing starts with an assumption – Frank is capable of solving this problem; I don't have to solve it for him.

- The skilful use of questions can not only activate the person's thinking but actually direct it along lines which we know will be productive.

- As managers, we have to invest our time in those problems and issues in regard to which our specific skills and insight will make a difference.

- The challenge is to bring our usage of time under our direct and conscious control – by making conscious, intelligent investment decisions.

- Reserve time for management by 'walking around'. It's your chance to wander around with an open mind and get a feel for what is happening.

- Moving in and out of situations is an important managerial skill. Linger just long enough to make a difference. And then keep moving.

- Look for opportunities to turn Fix-It problems into Do-It problems – to use the solving of a specific problem to improve things generally.

13
Problem-solving *en Groupe*

Rarely does a single person deal with a problem in isolation. Even just to get a handle on a problem, we may have to look at how it is seen by a number of different people – each coming at it from his or her own unique vantage point.

THE CHOICES

Deciding when and how to use the resources of the total group is not a simple case of yes or no. In the interests of keeping things simple, let's think in terms of three options:

- *Individual process.* As the manager, we assess the problem and announce our solution to the group.

- *Consultation.* We get the team together to consult with them around the issue but then make the final decision ourselves either then or at some later time.

- *Group process.* The team as a whole solves the problem.

The **individual approach** is clearly the best choice when:

- there is a tight deadline that has to be met
- the issue under consideration is confidential
- we are dealing with a crisis or emergency.

Or, indeed, when we – as manager – have a clear sense of where the group ought to be going and suspect that, left to their own resources, that's not at all where they would go.

The **group approach**, on the other hand, becomes essential when the enthusiastic commitment of each individual is vital to the success of our undertaking. Commitment flows from ownership, and ownership flows from involvement.

| Involvement | ▶ | Ownership | ▶ | Commitment |

The **consultative approach** is useful when specialist input is required. It is also useful when we need to find out where and how various people on the team are being affected.

There are times, too, when it makes sense to use the group or consultative approach because of certain other benefits which they offer . . .

THE BENEFITS OF WORKING TOGETHER

Sheer productivity – measured in terms of the quantity and quality of ideas produced – tends to be higher in a group.

Cross-fertilisation is the obvious benefit here. The interaction of ideas gets individuals thinking along slightly new and different lines. The presence of the two people from Marketing keeps the sales people on their toes. And so on.

Communication is another benefit. People who have to *implement* a solution will get off to a good start by having worked together during the earlier phases of the problem-solving process.

Risk-taking is a benefit. Groups are more likely to take risks than individuals because the risk-takers in the group swing the more cautious members over to their view. Or it may be that, because the pressure of individual accountability is removed, people feel freer to subscribe to a bolder course of action.

To summarise, working together encourages:

- generation of ideas
- cross-fertilisation
- communication
- risk-taking.

Four good reasons for using a consultative or group approach when appropriate.

LEADERSHIP BEHAVIOURS

There are *drawbacks* associated with the use of a group or consultative approach to problem-solving. The most obvious of these is sheer inefficiency.

'I hate meetings. They are a complete waste of time. Most of what needs to be said doesn't get said because people are afraid to come right out and say what's on their mind. As a result, we end up agreeing to things that we don't really agree with and it spoils the whole bloody day unless you're lucky enough to have a pub lunch scheduled for right after the meeting.'

That is not an uncommon view of the way group meetings don't work. And the reason for that happening is a lack of effective leadership.

At this point it might be helpful to list, briefly, certain fairly specific strategies which help keep a group on track. They don't all have to be provided by you, the manager, but as various points in virtually any group meeting, *someone* will have to supply them.

Agenda setting
This means helping the group decide what to talk about.

• 'Why don't we start by defining what we mean by strategic?'

Encouragement
Encouraging someone to speak up.

• 'Jack. Any comments about what Heather has proposed?'

Gate keeping
This means making sure that everyone gets a chance to talk.

• 'Jim, why don't you go first – and then Hilary, you can . . .'

Policing
Stepping in when someone else in the group is dominating the discussion.

Reflection
This gives the speaker a chance to hear their thoughts expressed aloud and perhaps expand upon them.

• 'If I understand you correctly, Linda, you think that it's the tone of his suggestion – not the content *per se* – which caused it to be rejected?'

Re-focusing

Re-focusing means getting the discussion back on track.

- 'I think we're drifting away from the main issue here. We agreed that Step One was to define the problem, and I'm not sure that we've done that yet.'

Topic changing

Initiating a change in topic. It might involve suggesting that we leave this for now and talk about something else and then come back to this later.

Problem identification

This means explaining the reasons for a problem that the group itself is experiencing.

The real key here is to identify the problem in process terms, so that it carries a suggestion of what can be done about it.

- 'I think the reason we're having trouble making progress is that we haven't really agreed on just how broad our mandate is. What I mean by that is...'

Summarising

It is very useful, as a means of moving a discussion forward to periodically summarise what has been said and what progress has been made.

Consensus testing

This contributes quite directly to helping the group arrive at a decision.

- 'Are we all agreed, then, that our mandate is to develop a list of options rather than actually make a decision.'

THE PROBLEM-SOLVING TEAM

Solving problems isn't just an important part of a manager's day-to-day work. It is also something that they have to help *other* people do effectively. It is now time to step back and look at just how well your organisation promotes and nurtures a high level of problem-solving effectiveness for their employees.

Let's look at some of the relevant problem-solving characteristics which we commonly find in high-performing organisations.

1. People feel confident

In the right environment where problem-solving *effectiveness* has taken hold the hesitant decision-maker is a bit more assured and purposeful.

People feel good about themselves. They have learned through experience that their ideas count. They aren't under pressure to get approval for every little decision they have to make.

2. They have a sense of mission

In the problem-solving organisation, people have a sense of purpose. They are not simply coming in every day to do their 'jobs'.

No, they have a mission. They work for an organisation that is helping to create and satisfy an important need in the marketplace.

- We are making the world's finest wrist-watches.

- We are making it safer for women to have babies.

- We are changing the way people think about pensions.

- We are developing a cure for lymphoma.

People are working together toward a common end. They still argue or come into conflict but the arguments are *meaningful* and are to do with important strategies rather than reflecting petty differences. There is, too, a spirit of invention in the air. A *can-do* feeling where people know that what they're doing is important.

3. People are pushing for results

Scratch the average worker deep enough, and you will find their real concern is with doing a good job.

But it's not the same as pushing for results.

The person who pushes for results is not satisfied until the bottleneck has been sorted out, until the decision has been made.

4. They have the freedom to make mistakes

The key thing here is that people recognise that making mistakes is part of the learning process.

American executive William T. Brady had this to say in 1959 about the importance of allowing people room to make mistakes.

'Sometimes we forget how eager we were to try out our new ideas. All our people, I'm sure, have new ideas, too. They're itching to take a crack at putting them into practice, to swim in a little deeper water and justify their membership on the team. Good. You give them the chance. But maybe the idea doesn't work out quite so well. If there's a reprimand, what happens? Every time that enterprising spirit is broken down even a little, every time that little spark of originality is snuffed out, we are choking off the very taproots of our organisation's precious fund of creativity.'

5. There is a sense of urgency in the air

When you watch a high-performing team in action, even when the work being done is not especially physical, there is a buzz, a sense that important things are being thought about and accomplished. There is a sense that time is of the essence, that we have a lot to do, that we have to move *quickly* on things.

6. People sort problems out themselves

People don't run to their superiors. They sort things out amongst themselves.

7. Communication is direct and non-stop

People go direct and communicate face-to-face rather than relying on formal channels. Formal meetings are brief and productive, and kept to a minimum. The telephone lines are in constant use. Brief e-mail messages take the place of lengthy letters and proposals. Computers are linked so that everyone has access to the same data.

8. Conflict is dealt with constructively

Conflicts are used in a positive way to help the team move forward.

A healthy team will not shy away from conflict that revolves around substantive *ideas*. It demonstrates that the quality of communication is honest and candid and that debate is not being cut off prematurely in the dubious interests of 'harmony' or 'team spirit'.

Likewise, managers aren't hesitant to clamp down on someone who has failed to deliver a promised result on time. But it's done through an honest expression of concern with a genuine shifting of attention to the issue of how we can prevent the problem from happening again.

9. Systems are results-driven

In an effective problem-solving organisation, there is a clear and disciplined emphasis on goals and performance, and part of this is a belief in doing things systematically and measuring results. But systems are not allowed to become ends in themselves. They serve as a vehicle for reaching goals.

Graeme Weir, manufacturing director for a Leamington-based producer of automotive components and one of our *Famous Five*, had this to say:

'There are some key numbers that we all have to know about because they tell us how we are doing. There are certain rules we all follow because then we don't go around tripping over one another's toes. There are certain policies that we all know have to be adhered to because they represent our commitment to a certain way of doing business. And then there are certain procedures and systems that we all use because they make life easier; they allow us to get things done faster and with less fuss and bother. But that's it. Beyond that, there aren't too many times during the day when you'll find someone doing something a certain way just because it's "supposed to be done that way". We expect people to think.'

10. The team possesses 'self-belief'

There is a belief that the team is capable of dealing with things. And it shows up in many ways.

There is a willingness to tackle problems head-on, to be brutally objective about customer perceptions and market strengths. People aren't defensive. They aren't afraid to really *dig into* issues and get at the truth.

CREATING THE RIGHT CLIMATE

A company won't get a lot of people demonstrating initiative and innovative spirit unless a climate capable of *nurturing* such qualities has been created.

Do we, as a company, make it easy for people to be effective problem-solvers? or are we putting obstacles in their way?

To answer that, we need to know what specific *organisational* things work for and against effective problem-solving.

What we have, in Figure 19, is a brief listing of elements which work for – or against – the creation of an effective problem-solving climate. The left-hand column works *for* problem-solving effectiveness. The right-hand column works *against* it.

Adapting to a No-No-No-No environment

Of the 15 items included in Figure 19, the following are especially important.

1. Intelligent risk-taking is encouraged.	Y ☐ ☐ N
People are encouraged to think boldly about things and take intelligent risks.	People learn quickly that it is better to err on the side of safety and caution.

2. New ideas are encouraged.	Y ☐ ☐ N
People are encouraged to come forward with new ideas and proposals.	People who try to put forth new ideas just end up feeling frustrated.

3. Mistakes are tolerated.	Y ☐ ☐ N
An honest mistake is tolerated, so long as you learn something from it.	Managers tend to come down hard on someone who has made a mistake.

4. There is room for initiative.	Y ☐ ☐ N
People are given lots of room to think for themselves and exercise initiative.	People are expected to follow rules and stay within the boundary lines of their job.

5. We communicate.	Y ☐ ☐ N
Communication is direct, immediate, and honest. We *talk* to one another.	There is too much reliance on formal channels, too much rumour and gossip.

6. Senior managers are in touch.	Y ☐ ☐ N
Senior managers have a good feel for what is happening at the lower levels.	Senior management is out of touch with the everyday reality of the organisation.

7. Financial results are shared.	Y ☐ ☐ N
People are kept well informed of the group's financial results. Nothing is hidden.	Information is shared on a need-to-know basis. Secrecy and confusion abound.

8. The overall direction is clear.	Y ☐ ☐ N
The mission is clear. The priorities are identified. People know what has to be done.	We don't have a tangible, coherent sense of direction for the team as a whole.

9. Accountabilities are clear.	Y ☐ ☐ N
Outcomes are tied to specific people. People now who is accountable for what.	Accountabilities are fuzzy, and there is lots of room for people to 'escape'.

10. Performance problems are tackled head-on.	Y ☐ ☐ N
Performance problems are dealt with in an immediate and above-board fashion.	Performance problems tend to be swept under the rug and allowed to linger on.

11. There is a sense of teamwork.	Y ☐ ☐ N
There is a sense of us all pulling together in a common direction.	There is little sense of us all pulling toward a common objective.

12. We're flexible.	Y ☐ ☐ N
We can get the right people dealing with the right problem at the right time.	Too often, our organisational structure hinders rather than facilitates problem-solving.

13. Decision-making is pushed down the ladder.	Y ☐ ☐ N
When a decision needs to be made, it gets made. One thing we *don't* do is pass the buck.	It's difficult to get a decision made. No one seems to want to step up to bat.

14. Decisions get made quickly.	Y ☐ ☐ N
Decision-making tends to be pushed down the ladder as far as possible.	Key decisions tend to be made by a select group at the top of the organisation.

15. We are customer-oriented.	Y ☐ ☐ N
It's not just an empty slogan. This is truly a customer-driven organisation.	We say we are customer-driven, but it's not reflected in our day-to-day practises.

Fig. 19. Creating the right problem-solving climate.

- Intelligent risk-taking is encouraged.
- New ideas are encouraged.
- Mistakes are tolerated.
- There is room for initiative.

> **If an honest look around tells us that we're working in a *No-No-No-No* environment, then we either have to leave or adapt.**

It is unlikely, unless we own or run the business, that we can do much to *change* the environment.

Adapting means you have to be willing to compromise and settle for something less than you had originally hoped for. It means accepting the need to sell your ideas, sound out key influencers in advance of decisions being tabled.

Adapting means you have to decide which battles are worth fighting and which aren't. If you're a perfectionist, or an idealist, or a self-styled radical, then you're in the wrong environment.

Adapting means you have to watch what you say and how you say it and to *whom* you say it and *when* you say it. Not being able to say without inhibition or constraint what is on your mind is an insidious form of pressure. Freedom of speech is one of the foundations of job satisfaction.

Climate surveys

The usefulness of a list such as the one in Figure 19 is demonstrated when we build it into a **climate survey**. This affords us a unique opportunity to see our organisation through the eyes of our people. And – if there are specific things that we are doing that hinders people giving us their best performance – then this helps us to take a look at them and decide what action to take.

HIRING PROBLEM-SOLVING TALENT

One of the most practical ways to foster effective problem-solving throughout the entire organisation is to recruit or promote people who possess problem-solving skills.

Not many companies do a good job on this front. We pay a lot of attention to qualifications, the right sort of background, enthusiasm and ambition. And we are influenced by the poise and communication skills a candidate displays during an interview.

But there are at least *six* specific qualities which we normally aren't very good at assessing:

- *Critical thinking.* Is this a person who will question conventional wisdom?

- *Incisiveness.* How skillful is this person at separating what *counts* in a situation from what is not so important?

- *Analytical skill.* Is the person good at not looking to move into action before the problem has been properly defined?

- *Judgement.* Are the person's analytical skills and technical knowledge blended with a willingness to rely on intuition when necessary?

- *Action orientation.* Is this someone who will move from analysis to action at the earliest possible opportunity?

- *Leadership.* Can they lead the way forward toward the solution, mobilising and energising other people, giving them a vision of the result we are after and a sense of confidence about us being able to get there?

The assessment of job candidates is still a primitive art.

Most large companies still rely on the traditional interview and personnel testing, and smaller firms often rely on the interview alone.

Common sense is often our best guide. *Microsoft*, for example, give a candidate a half-hour to look through a file outlining a problem and they grill them on the problem some time later. It's an effective test of the candidate's problem-solving ability and presentation skills.

SETTING A PERSONAL EXAMPLE

Perhaps the best way to encourage other people to be effective problem-solvers is to give them a good model to emulate.

If you step in and do people's thinking for them or dismiss a far-fetched idea as impractical rather than exploring its possibilities you're setting the wrong example.

Here are the things you want to be able to say about yourself:

- I'm willing to tolerate an honest mistake so long as the other person has learned something from it.

- I expect people to act independently and display initiative, and they know that.

- I actively encourage people to think boldly, to *challenge* conventional wisdom.

- I have introduced 'brainstorming' as a way to help the team think creatively about things.

- I don't want people agreeing with everything I say. If they don't agree with something, I want to hear about it.

- I am willing to change my mind on a key issue if someone can give me a logical reason for doing so.

- I try to help people think things through rather than just giving them advice or telling them what to do.

And...

- People know these things about me.

- I've demonstrated them time and time again.

KEY POINTS

- Rarely – these days – does a single person deal with a problem in isolation. More often than not, problem-solving involves quite a few different people.

- Deciding when and how to use the resources of the total group is not a simple case of yes or no. In practice, there is a range of options.

- An individual approach works best when there is a tight deadline that has to be met, the issue is confidential, or we are dealing with a crisis.

- The group approach is essential when the enthusiastic commitment of each and every individual is vital to the success of our undertaking.

- The consultative approach is useful when specialist input is required or when we need to find out how various people are being affected.

- Generation of ideas, cross-fertilisation, communication, and risk-taking – these are four of the benefits from using a consultative or group approach.

- The biggest drawback in using a group approach is its sheer inefficiency, and the single biggest cause of inefficiency is a lack of effective leadership.

- There are 10 characteristics that we see in high-performing teams and organisations – reflecting a high level of problem-solving effectiveness.

- Organisational climate can either nurture – or dampen – the initiative and innovativeness and resourcefulness with which people tackle problems.

- So, too can the personal example that each and every manager sets for his or her people. We have to give them a model that they can emulate.

Further Reading

Creative Management, Jane Henry (ed.) (London: SAGE Publications, 1991).

Making Decisions: How to develop effective skills for making good decisions, Dean Juniper (How To Books, 1998).

Thinking Strategically, Craig Loehle (Cambridge: Cambridge University Press, 1996).

The Fifth Discipline, Peter M. Senge (New York: Doubleday/ Currency, 1990).

Successful Intelligence, Robert J. Sternberg (New York: Simon & Schuster, 1996).

And the best reading material of all . . . the business section of the *Times* or one of the other major London broadsheets. There is no better way to learn about problem-solving than to keep abreast of what real people and real companies are doing to meet the enormous challenges of doing business in today's volatile and brutally competitive environment.

Index

MAKING DECISIONS
How to develop effective skills for making good decisions

Dean Juniper

If we are to make maximum use of every available choice opportunity in our business and personal lives, it is vital that we sharpen and focus our decision-making skills. We also need insight into the decision-making styles of ourselves and others, so that we can shape our performance and adjust our thinking to suit changing circumstances. Dean Juniper has brought together a career-long experience of educational guidance and counselling psychology to bear upon this, his latest book. It explores and summarises all the skills necessary for effective thinking in action.

168pp. illus. 1 85703 296 9.

MAKING EFFECTIVE SPEECHES
How to motivate and persuade in every business situation

John Bowden

Written specifically for people competing in today's tough business world, this book shows you how to get that competitive edge by becoming a comfortable, effective speaker, equipped with the skills necessary to deliver dynamic business speeches. You will learn how to communicate your ideas, motivate employees, influence opinions, and much more. Business speeches are important – they must succeed. This book will help turn your speeches into personal and corporate triumphs. John Bowden MSc has over 25 years' experience as a manager in industry, and as a professional trainer and senior lecturer in communication skills. He is author of *Making a Wedding Speech* and *Writing a Report* in this series.

128pp. 1 85703 291 8.

CONDUCTING EFFECTIVE INTERVIEWS
How to find out what you need to know and achieve the right results

Ann Dobson

Whether you are interviewing a job applicant, dealing with disciplinary procedures or organising a decision-making session, this book will provide you with all the information you need to achieve your aims. Part 1 offers a step-by-step guide to the general principles of interviewing and Part 2 illustrates the various types of interviews you may be involved with in your working life.

128pp. illus. 1 85703 223 3.

MANAGING THROUGH PEOPLE
How to get the best from your most valuable resource

John Humphries

People are the most valuable resource of any organisation, and managing people successfully is the surest way for an organisation to achieve its objectives. *Managing Through People*, originally titled *How to Manage People at Work*, has been fully revised to take into account the changing role of managers, for example how to support and coordinate a non-standard workforce, such as those working from home on a freelance basis. In fact this book covers, in one handy volume, every aspect of people management that today's business leaders require. 'Highly informative, reliable, comprehensive and user-friendly – has tackled an extremely wide subject ably and well.' *Progress* (NEBS Management Association). John Humphries BSc has 20 years' professional experience as a management trainer and is an NVQ assessor.

160pp illus. 1 85703 271 3. 3rd edition.